GENESIS OF THE PHARAOHS

TOBY WILKINSON

GENESIS OF THE PHARAOHS

*Dramatic new discoveries rewrite
the origins of ancient Egypt*

with 87 illustrations, 25 in color

Thames & Hudson

For Georgina

First published in hardcover in the United States of America in 2003 by
Thames & Hudson Inc., 500 Fifth Avenue, New York, New York 10110

thamesandhudsonusa.com

Library of Congress Catalog Card Number 2002110322
ISBN 0-500-05122-4

Printed and bound in Slovenia by DZS

CONTENTS

ACKNOWLEDGMENTS

7

INTRODUCTION

9

1 THE DESERT SPEAKS
Making the Discoveries

12

2 THE SANDS OF TIME
Dating the Rock Art

54

3 HUNTERS AND HERDERS
Unmasking the Artists

83

4 BEFORE THE PHARAOHS
Life in Predynastic Egypt

113

5 SHIPS OF THE DESERT
The Birth of the Egyptian Religion

134

6 CRADLE OF CIVILIZATION
Re-thinking Ancient Egyptian Origins

162

POSTSCRIPT

196

MAPS AND TABLE

198

BIBLIOGRAPHY AND GUIDE TO FURTHER READING

201

SOURCES OF ILLUSTRATIONS

204

INDEX

206

ACKNOWLEDGMENTS

*T*he archaeological and natural wonders of Egypt's Eastern Desert might well have remained hidden to me had it not been for a chance conversation with Mike and Maggie Morrow. Their enthusiasm and encouragement prompted my involvement in the Eastern Desert survey, leading to the new discoveries presented in this book. I am profoundly grateful to them for this initial stimulus, and for many subsequent discussions on the petroglyphs and their significance. Navigating a path through previously inaccessible terrain requires detailed maps, strategic thinking and a certain flair for desert exploration. Dr Peter Cherry provided all three and, just as important, a dogged determination to discover and record as many sites of rock art as possible within the limited time available to our expeditions. I should like to thank him, and fellow explorers Geoff Phillipson, Tony Judd, Kevin Wright and Gene Greenwood, for their companionship in the desert and for many lively debates around the camp fire.

The credit for reawakening interest in Egypt's Eastern Desert and its remarkable prehistoric rock art must go to David Rohl. Back in 1996, he made pioneering trips into this inhospitable terrain, finding navigable routes through the hills and dry valleys to some of the most important sites of early human activity. His vision paved the way for the expeditions which followed. These were made possible by the logistical brilliance of Ancient World Tours, assisted by Pan Arab Tours and its expert drivers. My particular thanks go to Michael Ackroyd, Janet Wilton and Peter Allingham at Ancient World Tours; and to Ahmed Mousa and Hamdy Mahdy of Pan Arab Tours.

Away from the rigours of the Eastern Desert, I have been fortunate to receive help and advice from a number of sources during my research for this book. The Committee of the Egypt Exploration Society kindly gave me permission to consult Winkler's original expedition notebooks, and to publish, for the first time, the precise details of his travels in the Eastern Desert. I should like to express my thanks to the EES and to its Secretary, Dr Patricia Spencer, for her generous assistance. My thanks are also due to Dr Sylvia Peuckert for reading through Winkler's notebooks with me, and for important information about his early life and work. Professor Willeke Wendrich and her husband kindly shared information about the present-day inhabitants of the Eastern Desert. The editorial and production staff at Thames & Hudson have shown unfailing enthusiasm for this project, for which I am most grateful. I owe a particularly big debt of gratitude to Dr Kate Spence for the splendid line drawings which accompany the text.

On a personal note, the genesis of this book occurred not long after the birth of my niece, Georgina. Its ideas have grown as she has grown, and she never ceases to be an inspiration. May she flourish as the civilization of ancient Egypt flourished. I dedicate this book to her with love and pride.

INTRODUCTION

Where did the ancient Egyptians come from? The question has intrigued generations of scholars, tourists, and armchair travellers. Was civilization brought to the Nile Valley by aliens from outer space? by refugees from Atlantis? by invaders from other lands? or did civilization develop over a long period of time within Egypt itself? The first three theories make good television, and sell lots of books; but most Egyptologists, and most thinking members of the general public, favour the last theory. It makes most sense of the available evidence, and it does not require the suspension of disbelief, as exciting as that may be on occasions. And yet… Nagging doubts have always remained about the origins of ancient Egypt, caused above all by gaps in the evidence.

We all recognize ancient Egyptian art and religion when we see them. From the time of Tutankhamun, when pharaohs built their tombs in the Valley of the Kings, the characteristic features of Egyptian culture can be traced back through the New Kingdom, Middle Kingdom and Old Kingdom to the very dawn of Egyptian history at the beginning of the First Dynasty. Thanks to recent excavations, we can push ancient Egyptian origins even further back, into the prehistoric period that preceded the First Dynasty. Yet there is still a major gap in the record, still a 'missing link'. So many of the aspects that distinguish pharaonic culture seem to have come into being quite suddenly, without any discernible predecessors. It is this void in the archaeological record that provides such fertile ground for writers' imaginations. The void can at last be filled.

The origins of ancient Egyptian civilization have come to light in the most unlikely of places. In the heart of the Eastern Desert, between the Nile Valley and the Red Sea, the rocks tell a story of a people who, 6,000 years ago, sowed the seeds that were to become Egypt of the pharaohs. At dozens of sites throughout this now inhospitable region, the early inhabitants left a remarkable legacy in the form of rock art. The pictures (known to archaeologists as 'petroglyphs') tell us about their way of life, their environment and their religious beliefs. Many of the images foreshadow the classic repertoire of ancient Egyptian art; and yet they were carved 3,500 years before the pharaohs built their decorated tombs in the Valley of the Kings. This book sets out to trace the discovery of these remarkable ancient records, to date them, and to identify the artists who made them. As our story unfolds, we will travel back in time to a remarkable environment; we will reveal its ancient inhabitants and their distinctive way of life; and we will finally be able to answer the questions of where, when and how ancient Egypt began.

~ · ~ · ~

On 11 December 2000, my team of desert travellers and I arrived back from Egypt, exhausted but elated. We had just completed a one-week exploration of the Eastern Desert, discovering more than thirty sites of prehistoric rock art. This was a record, surpassing the efforts of all the previous Eastern Desert Survey expeditions. Even more exciting, this treasure-house of images had never been recorded before. Indeed, some of the scenes may not have been seen since they were first made, 6,000 years ago. The importance of what we had found slowly dawned on us, as we discussed and debated our discoveries. Not only did the images constitute a unique and spectacular artistic heritage; they also provided startling new evidence for the origins of ancient Egyptian civilization. The genesis of the pharaohs would have to be rewritten.

Through a personal contact of a team member, Britain's *Guardian* newspaper learned of our exciting discoveries and ran a story soon after Christmas 2000. That was just the beginning. The story sparked immediate and intense media interest in our work. Newspapers from Australia, Switzerland, Germany and Italy telephoned for interviews, quotes, and for access to pictures of the newly discovered rock art. Britain's *Daily Mail* decided to follow the *Guardian* article with a double-page spread the very next day, prompting a further rash of enquiries from international press agencies and satellite television companies. The telephone and email lines buzzed, almost continuously, for several weeks. During the following months, I gave a series of lectures and study days across Britain, bringing the Eastern Desert rock art to the attention of scholars and the wider public. The reaction was universal: these dramatic new discoveries force us to rethink the origins of ancient Egypt, and they deserve the widest possible recognition.

This book aims to meet that challenge. I hope all who read about our wonderful discoveries will marvel, as we have, at the sophistication of Egypt's prehistoric people; at their capacity for great art; and at the new light which the desert images shed on the beginnings of the world's greatest ancient civilization.

1

THE DESERT SPEAKS
Making the Discoveries

Nothing prepares you for your first encounter with the desert. Sand and bare rock as far as the eye can see, boundless skies, and no other living being in sight: in its silence, its mystery and majesty, the Eastern Desert of Egypt is unlike anywhere else in the world. It is a lonely and isolated place, and yet somehow strangely comforting; for the natural world feels closer here than it ever does in the largely man-made environment of the West. Signs of life are few, and yet the desert possesses a palpable atmosphere: an air of great antiquity laced with long-forgotten beliefs.

Unlike the Sahara to the west of the River Nile, here to the east the desert is predominantly a rocky landscape (Plate 1). Dry valleys (wadis in Arabic), scoured out by rivers in antiquity, cut swathes through the jagged hills. The terrain is difficult and confusing. Until the advent of modern satellite navigation, finding a way through this region was practically impossible without the help of local guides and a sure-footed camel. Food and water are scarce – non-existent in places – and surviving in this wilderness is tough. Little wonder, then, that few Europeans had ever succeeded in penetrating the forbidding interior of Egypt's Eastern Desert. The accolade for being the first archaeologist to brave the journey eastwards from the Nile Valley seems to belong to the Russian scholar Golenischeff. As early as 1887, he travelled through the Wadi Hammamat, and his account of the expedition first awakened interest in this remote region; in particular, it alerted Egyptologists to the abundant hieroglyphic mining inscriptions at the siltstone quarries of the Black Mountains.

The first Egyptologist to take a lively interest in the prehistoric rock art of the region was the Englishman Arthur Weigall. From an early age, Weigall seemed destined for a glittering career. He did sufficiently well at school to win a place at New College, Oxford, and he went up to begin his studies in 1900. Unbeknown to Weigall, that very same year, a few hundred miles away in Germany, a boy was born, by the name of Hans Winkler, who was to dominate the story of desert exploration in Egypt. But that was still some time in the future. By 1900, Weigall himself had become fascinated by Egypt and its ancient treasures. Egyptian archaeology had recently entered a new era, thanks to the scientific methods practised by Flinders Petrie. Revered after his death as the founding father of Egyptian archaeology, Petrie had brought a much-needed and long-overdue professionalism to the subject. He believed that the duty of the archaeologist was not merely to seek for treasure (as so many of his predecessors had done), but to record and publish even the smallest detail that might shed new light on the past. To this end, from 1896, Petrie had brought out a series of – for the time – exemplary excavation reports. Published almost annually, at the close of each season's excavations, the books featured drawings of pottery and small finds, comparative tables of graves and their contents, and a wealth of other information. They truly broke the mould of archaeological reports, and must have opened the eyes of the young Weigall to the potential of archaeology in general, and Egyptian archaeology in particular.

In 1900, the year Weigall went up to Oxford, Petrie published the first volume of results from his pioneering excavations at Abydos. This site in Upper Egypt was where the kings of Egypt's First Dynasty had chosen to be buried. Petrie's re-excavation of their tombs (which had been looted by a series of earlier treasure-hunters, masquerading as archaeologists) revealed startling new insights into the very beginning of ancient Egyptian history. We can judge the impact *Royal Tombs of the First Dynasty* must have had on Weigall. For, less than six months later, he abruptly left Oxford, abandoning his studies to join Petrie as his assistant on the staff of the Egypt Exploration Fund (EEF). The EEF was the main British organization conducting excavations in Egypt, something it had been doing with increasing success since it was first founded in 1882. The early years of the twentieth century were, in many ways, the glory days of the EEF, with some of Egypt's most important archaeological sites being opened up for the first time. It was in the midst of this exciting activity that Weigall now found himself.

Weigall took to Egyptology like a duck to water. His first fieldwork experience was with Petrie at Abydos, helping to clear the remaining royal tombs of the First and Second Dynasties, and beginning excavation of the early town and temple sites. But Weigall did not remain a humble assistant for long. Within just four years of joining the EEF, he had risen rapidly through the ranks, to be appointed Inspector-General of Antiquities for the Egyptian government, at the age of just twenty-five. This was the most important position in Egyptology within Egypt itself (still under strong British colonial influence). It gave Weigall access to every archaeological site, and virtual carte blanche to explore and excavate wheresoever he chose. Given the abundance of alluring monuments at his disposal, his early choices were surprising. In 1907 he undertook a survey of Egyptian Nubia, the stretch of the Nile Valley south of Aswan. To European archaeologists, as to the ancient Egyptians themselves, Nubia was a strange and exotic land, not quite part of pharaonic Egypt. Weigall's interest seemed to signal an attraction for the wilder and more inaccessible parts of his new domain.

His second survey expedition went even further in this direction: leaving the familiar Nile Valley behind him in November that same year, Weigall set out on a journey into the wilderness of the Upper Egyptian deserts. He travelled from Luxor with three English companions, a servant, a guide, two guards, a chief camelman and a dozen further camelmen. The nine highest-ranking members of the expedition travelled by camel, while the lowly camelmen went on foot. The whole caravan comprised no fewer than twenty-three camels, fourteen of them dedicated to carrying tents and supplies. Weigall's account of his journey must rank as one of the classic stories from the early days of Egyptology. He vividly conjures up not only the sense of adventure, the haunting landscapes and atmosphere of Egypt, but also the supreme confidence of the European colonialists in those days of Empire:

The day was cool, and a strong invigorating breeze raced past us…Before us, as we crossed the fields, the sunlit desert lay stretched behind the soft green of the tamarisks which border its edge. Away to the right the three peaks of the limestone hills…rose into the sunlight; and to the left one could discern the distant ranges behind which we were to penetrate.

On reaching the outskirts of the small town of Qus, Weigall's party turned eastwards, heading into the desert, along the Wadi Hammamat towards their ultimate destination, the siltstone quarries at the heart of the Black Mountains. Despite the attendance of guides and a servant, the conditions were far from comfortable. Weigall clearly suffered the same deprivations as countless earlier generations of travellers in this inhospitable terrain:

Setting out on a journey towards the Red Sea one rides on camel-back over this rolling plain, with the sun bombarding one's helmet from above and the wind charging it from the flank; and, as noonday approaches, one often looks in vain for a rock under which to find shade.

Weigall's progress by camel along the Wadi Hammamat was slow and deliberate (Fig. 1). Those were the early days of the motor car, and the terrain was still difficult, if not impassable, for road vehicles. Nevertheless, Weigall made an uncanny prediction about future travellers in the Eastern Desert. He wrote:

1 *Arthur Weigall in the Eastern Desert. Taken in the early 1900s, this photograph is a wonderful evocation of the Edwardian spirit of adventure and exploration.*

In the future one may picture the energetic tourist leaving his Luxor or Cairo hotel, whirling over the open plains where now one crawls, rushing through the valleys in whch the camel-rider lingers, penetrating to the remote ruins and deserted workings and emerging breathless on to the golden coast of the sea.

In 1907, however, a camel train covered only about thirty miles a day; but the slow speed of transport must have been compensated by the commanding view from a camel's back, and the ability to stick close to the edge of the cliffs, scrutinizing the rock surface for petroglyphs. Weigall made his first discovery at Qusur el-Banat (see MAP 2, p. 199), the same isolated rock that subsequent expeditions would also stop at and record on their way from the Nile Valley into the Eastern Desert. Further east, Weigall also noted a series of Middle Kingdom hieroglyphic inscriptions just before a sharp right-hand turn in the wadi's course. Yet he failed to note, or even notice, a dramatic collection of prehistoric petroglyphs just a couple of hundred yards beyond. It is easy to imagine why he missed this particular rock art site: his attention was already focussed on the Black Mountains looming in the distance. He clearly wished to press on and reach his ultimate destination, without taking too much time or trouble to search for petroglyphs, in the way our expedition would nearly a century later. Weigall reached the siltstone quarries, only the third ever Egyptologist to do so. On returning to the Nile Valley he had clearly succumbed to the Eastern Desert's peculiar spell:

Had I now in my two open hands pearls, diamonds, and rubies, how gladly would I give them – or some of them – for the sight of the misty mountains of the Eastern Desert, and for the feel of the sharp air of the hills!

Indeed, it would not be long before he felt drawn 'to be off again, "over the hills and far away," into the solitary splendour of the desert'.

The very next year, 1908, Weigall, accompanied this time by his redoubtable wife, set out from the ancient city of Elkab in Upper Egypt with their attendants and camels. To judge from his account, he must have taken the same route as our own expedition in 1999. Turning off the main north–south road opposite the town of Edfu, Weigall entered the Eastern Desert along the Wadi Barramiya. This was to be the only area he explored, for his goal was not the discovery of petroglyphs but a visit to the remote, New Kingdom temple of pharaoh

Seti I at Kanais. We can well imagine what must have passed through Weigall's mind when he first came to this haunting spot, with its rock-cut shrine, its ancient well, and its Roman fort. But these later remains, even the temple's brightly coloured reliefs, do not seem to have interested Weigall as much as the rock art pecked into the nearby cliff face. He quickly realized that some images were prehistoric in date, and that the site of Kanais had therefore been one of religious importance for thousands of years. Unlike some later desert explorers, Weigall seems to have been in no doubt that the petroglyphs were the work of Egyptian artists, working very much within the traditions of Egyptian religious imagery. He was clearly fascinated by the intriguing images of boats, of so many different shapes and sizes; for he made detailed copies of them. When these were published in 1909, they were the first accurate reproductions of Egypt's earliest art. Sad to say, Egyptology was too preoccupied with the ongoing work in the Valley of the Kings – soon to yield clues that would eventually lead Carter and Carnarvon to the tomb of Tutankhamun – to take much notice of Weigall's discoveries in the remote Eastern Desert. They would have to await the attentions of another, equally determined adventurer, a generation later.

In the winter of 1936–37, and again the following year, the German scholar Hans Winkler travelled through the deserts to the east and west of the Nile, searching for clues about Egypt's earliest inhabitants. His sponsor was the Englishman Sir Robert Mond, chemist, successful businessman and lover of all things Egyptian. Mond was keen to advance research into ancient Egypt; and the origins of that great civilization particularly interested him. Perhaps he had heard travellers' tales about strange and wonderful images deep in the desert. Or perhaps, aware of the numerous petroglyphs that decorated the mouths of wadis close to the Nile, Mond had a hunch that the upper reaches of the same wadis held yet greater treasures. In any case, in 1936, he put his considerable financial backing behind a new expedition. Its objective was to discover and record rock art in the further reaches of the Western and (especially) Eastern Deserts. All he needed was a determined and resourceful Egyptologist, someone who would not baulk at spending several months in uncomfortable and inhospitable terrain in the name of archaeology. Hans Winkler was that person.

Born in Bremerhaven, northern Germany, on 14 February 1900, Winkler's early life was deeply affected by his country's defeat in the First World War. The spiralling inflation that racked Germany in the 1920s had many casualties, Winkler's family among them. The young Winkler was academically gifted, but to help pay for his studies he had to work for a time as a miner. This experience seems to have coloured his politics, and he briefly joined the German Communist Party, a decision that affected the rest of his career. Enrolling at the University of Tübingen, he studied under the oriental scholar Enno Littmann and graduated in 1925. He continued his studies at Tübingen until 1933, when he was dismissed from his post and prevented from taking up another academic post at Göttingen University. Germany had fallen under the spell of the National Socialists and their charismatic leader Adolf Hitler. Hitler was elected German Chancellor in 1933, and almost instantly the purge began. Because of Winkler's temporary dalliance with Communist politics, and compounded by his marriage to an Armenian wife, he fell foul of the Nazi ideologues. The myth of 'Aryan' supremacy was, none the less, to haunt Winkler's work for the rest of his life.

His early interest was in the history of religion, but during the middle years of the 1930s he became increasingly attracted to contemporary folk culture, especially the culture of Egypt. The science of anthropology – the study of human societies – was a relatively new one; but it had become fashionable in Europe, particularly among the colonial powers of England, France and Germany. In the colonies of the great African continent – divided up between, and squabbled over by the European powers – anthropologists were often uncomfortably close to colonial administrators. There was a great divide in anthropology itself between those who believed passionately in the essential unity of humankind, and those who took the opposite view: that certain people, certain races, were inherently superior or inferior. This latter viewpoint suited the colonial mindset, and it struck a particular chord in Nazi Germany, where the regime was increasingly obsessed with the twisted ideology of racial supremacy.

Meanwhile, Winkler's work in the villages of Upper Egypt brought him into close contact with the various peoples of the Nile Valley and its hinterland. It was also at this time that he first came into contact with rock art, and began to appreciate its importance for Egyptian prehistory. In 1932 Winkler took the opportunity of a lifetime: a journey along the Wadi Hammamat from Guft on the banks of the Nile to Quseir on the shores of the Red Sea. Riding through the Black Mountains, Winkler marvelled at the hieroglyphic inscriptions in the siltstone quarries, but he was even more struck by what he saw on the return journey. Just beyond a sharp bend in the course of the wadi, at a place the locals called, appropriately, Abu Kua ('father of the elbow'), Winkler came across strange images pecked into the rock. To his eyes, they looked 'un-Egyptian', but there could be no doubt about what they represented: people wearing feathers in their hair. These pictures from a long-vanished age imprinted themselves on Winkler's imagination. As soon as another opportunity to study the petroglyphs presented itself, he seized it. So, in 1934, when he was once again spending time near Guft, carrying out ethnographic fieldwork, he set off by camel to take a second, longer look at the Abu Kua inscriptions. Accompanied by a Bedouin guide, Winkler spent eight days searching the neighbouring wadis. The sheer quantity of petroglyphs was amazing. Here, in the desert, lay unexpected clues about the beginnings of ancient Egyptian civilization. Winkler was well and truly hooked. The study of these remarkable ancient records was now set to dominate his career. Later the same year, Winkler published the first of his seminal works on Egyptian folk culture. This was followed two years later by another book on the same topic, but it was to be his last publication on the subject that had brought him to Egypt in the first place. Perhaps because he was banned from academic appointments in Germany by the Nazi regime, Winkler took the momentous decision that year to accept an invitation from a British archaeological expedition to Egypt. With his intimate knowledge of the Eastern Desert and its secrets,

Winkler was the obvious choice to lead the Robert Mond Expedition. Indeed, it seems that Winkler positively relished the prospect of new discoveries that the expedition offered. And so, towards the end of 1936, he began his epic series of journeys that was to open up a new window on the world of ancient Egypt.

Setting out in November 1936, Winkler left the Nile Valley at the town of Guft (ancient Coptos) and started eastwards along the Wadi Hammamat. The first site of rock art he encountered – which he duly labelled as Site 1 – was the prominent outcrop of rocks on the northern side of the wadi, where Weigall had stopped some twenty-nine years previously. Winkler recorded this site, known to the locals as the Qusur el-Banat, in his notebook on 20 November 1936. From there, he pushed further east, still following the Hammamat road, recording Sites 2 to 7 during the next week. After a week's break, perhaps to re-stock his supplies, he set out again along the narrower valleys to the north of the Wadi Hammamat, reaching Site 12 (at the mouth of the Wadi el-Atwani) on 6 December and the spectacular Site 15 three days later. Winkler's progress seems to have been quite slow, even considering that he travelled by camel. He must have been making a meticulous search of the rock face at every point, noting down petroglyphs which seemed particularly significant. It is telling that his unpublished notebooks are full of sketches – not of the fantastic boats and hunting scenes he discovered, but of later Bedouin, Coptic and Arab signs. These fascinated Winkler, and not only because he had a detailed knowledge of Egyptian folk culture. The signs which he took greatest pains to copy were those which resembled the swastika – the ancient Indian device, adopted by the Nazis as a symbol of their 'Aryan' ancestry and supposed racial supremacy. For the modern reader of Winkler's notebooks, this preoccupation with the swastika is uncomfortable. Nazi ideology had clearly imprinted itself on Winkler's mind. He appears to have been repelled yet strangely attracted by it, at the same time. During his many lonely months in the Eastern Desert, he seems to have grappled with the implications of racial supremacy, seeking evidence to prove or disprove the associated theory that the great civilization of ancient Egypt was the creation, not of 'savage' Africans, but of enlightened invaders from the 'Aryan' world to the east. This obsession would also colour Winkler's interpretation of the most intriguing petroglyphs – as we shall see later.

After another week's break, Winkler set out to explore the wadis to the south of the Hammamat road. It was on 20 December that he came to his eighteenth new site, a site so rich in drawings that it was worth a second visit on Boxing Day 1936. From Winkler's preliminary publication, Site 18 looks to have been one of the most impressive and important of rock art sites in the entire Eastern Desert. In addition to the usual hunting scenes, it also featured two early royal names, and the earliest example of a ruler wearing the red crown – in later, pharaonic times, one of the two principal crowns worn by Egyptian kings (Figs 23 and 24). With a discovery such as this, it is little wonder that Winkler allowed himself only a short Christmas break before setting out again on his journey of discovery.

Between Christmas and New Year 1936, Winkler explored the Wadi Qash and Wadi Zeidun, recording only four new sites of rock art. However, the New Year's season, which began after a week's break on 8 January 1937, was to be much more productive. In the space of just two days, Winkler discovered no fewer than seventeen new sites. Most of them were scattered along both sides of the Wadi Mineh. This had been an important route even in pharaonic times, as it led to one of the few reliable sources of fresh water deep in the Eastern Desert. Winkler was uncharacteristically hasty in his recording of the Wadi Mineh rock art sites, confusing some of them in his preliminary publication and inaccurately describing the location of others. The reason for this unusual lapse of concentration seems to have been the promise of a yet more spectacular site in a neighbouring valley, the Wadi Abu Wasil. Winkler must have had an inkling of this site, and its potential importance. Perhaps his Bedouin guides had mentioned its existence. It was certainly worth rushing to see. On both sides of the narrow valley, some of the most impressive rock art in the entire Eastern Desert decorated the cliff faces. So extensive was the site (Winkler's Site 26) that he spent nearly a week recording and photographing the petroglyphs. Only on 16 January did he set off again in search of further sites. He found two more in a nearby wadi before deciding to leave the Eastern Desert on 17 January 1937.

This time, the indefatigable explorer allowed himself a two-week break in the pleasant greenness of the Nile Valley. Re-supplied and re-invigorated, he set off again on 1 February to explore the sandy wastes of the Western Desert, in the mountains behind the Valley of the Kings. In the course of the next two months, he found just ten sites: important in their own right, but slender pickings compared with the riches of the Eastern Desert. Ironically, it was during his explorations in the Western Desert that he began to take more of an interest in the drawings of boats, even though they had been much more abundant in the Eastern Desert. Winkler must, surely, have sensed that there was a great deal more to find in the hills and wadis to the east of the Nile, but he was never to return there. For personal tragedy intervened in the cruellest way. In early April 1937, he completed his mammoth first season of desert travels. Over the course of four-and-a-half months, Winkler had travelled more extensively in Egypt's deserts than any other European before him. He had recorded an unexpected and spectacular variety of rock art in some of the most impenetrable terrain on earth. Just eight weeks after he hung up his desert boots, his beloved wife Hayastan died back home in Geneva, aged only thirty-six. When the news filtered through to Egypt, Winkler must have been grief-stricken. He hadn't seen Hayastan for half a year, and now she was gone. In his eagerness to strike out again into the desert, into ever more unexplored and inhospitable regions, one can sense his wish to escape the world and its agonies. So, on 22 November that year, Winkler set out once again into the Western Desert, pushing further and further south and west towards the dramatic terrain of the Gilf el-Kebir plateau. His discoveries here, in Egypt's furthest southwestern corner, over the next two months included rock paintings left behind by the Sahara's earliest inhabitants. They opened up yet another window on Africa's prehistoric past; but they are another story.

Thankfully for later generations of Egyptologists, Winkler kept reasonably detailed records of his discoveries. He noted the location of each rock art site, and described the general composition of each scene. Using chalk to highlight the inscriptions (Plate 4), he supplemented his written descriptions with large numbers of photographs. Winkler's photographic archive is still an invaluable resource for today's travellers to the Eastern Desert. It is held by the Egypt Exploration Society of London (as the Egypt Exploration Fund had become in 1919), together with his original expedition notebooks. Although working for the British Robert Mond Expedition, Winkler kept notes in his native German. This, combined with his handwriting and the difficult conditions under which he made his notes, make the books particularly difficult to decipher. Even with access to his sketches and the accompanying photographs (some of which were published in his preliminary reports), many questions about Winkler's expedition remain unanswered. For example, it is unclear how he navigated his way through the tortuous wadis of the Eastern Desert. His maps were adequate, but by no means detailed. Almost certainly, he would have relied on local Bedouin guides. Indeed, most of the sites he visited would have been well-known by the local, semi-nomadic inhabitants. In general, the greatest concentrations of petroglyphs are located in shady or sheltered spots, out of the heat of the blinding midday sun. Such refuges have been used since time immemorial; several rock art sites had evidently seen continuous use over many thousands of years, and were still being added to by the camel-herders of Winkler's time. It is telling that some of the best rock art – including the vast number of sites that our own expedition was to discover in the Wadi Umm Salam – escaped Winkler's attention entirely. The likeliest explanation is that these areas were simply unknown to his guides.

Even though he made little reference to boat petroglyphs in his notebooks, Winkler must have pondered the significance of these intriguing images. What, he must have wondered, were pictures of boats doing, hundreds of miles from the Nile or the Red Sea? Some of the boats were of a distinctive square shape, with a high prow and stern.

These reminded Winkler of similar boats illustrated on objects from Mesopotamia. Could there be a connection? In Winkler's mind a bold theory began to emerge.

Other archaeologists of the time had already speculated that a 'master race' of Eastern Invaders had been responsible for the creation of ancient Egyptian civilization. How else to account for the apparently sudden explosion of creativity and artistry at the beginning of the First Dynasty? In the 1930s, knowledge of Egypt's predynastic civilization was still in its infancy. The science of radiocarbon dating – which allows archaeologists to date ancient remains independently and with considerable accuracy – had yet to be invented. There was no objective evidence to decide whether certain important aspects of civilization had been developed first in Egypt or Mesopotamia. Furthermore, the theory of a 'master race', responsible for bringing civilization to primitive peoples, struck a chord in 1930s Europe – and not only in Nazi Germany. Winkler's discoveries in the Eastern Desert seemed to provide concrete proof for his colleagues' speculation: here were the drawings of the Eastern Invaders themselves. The petroglyphs of square boats must be records of their maritime expeditions to Egypt. Landing on the Red Sea coast, they had followed the broad wadis leading westwards to the Nile Valley. There, encountering a primitive prehistoric people, they had brought civilization and culture to the land of Egypt, ushering in the age of the pharaohs.

Winkler's theory, very much a product of his time, was nevertheless set to dominate discussions of ancient Egyptian origins for the next two decades. His own future as a pioneering Egyptologist looked bright; but, once again, fate cruelly intervened. The same fascination with the idea of a master race that informed Winkler's theory had led Europe to the brink. In September 1939, Britain declared war on Germany. Winkler was drafted into the German army, leaving the world of Egyptology far behind. His preliminary publications on the Eastern Desert rock art – two volumes of brief notes and photographs entitled *Rock Drawings of Upper Egypt* – were to be his last. In 1945, just a few weeks before the end of the war, Winkler was shot dead on active service in Poland. His work was to remain largely forgotten for the next fifty years, as Europe picked itself up from the war and Egyptologists focussed their attention on the rich pickings of the Nile Valley.

Interest in Egypt's prehistoric rock art flickered again briefly in the 1960s. In 1960–61, Winkler's fellow countryman Walther Resch spent several months in Egypt, looking for new sites along the Wadi Barramiya where Winkler had never ventured. Resch succeeded in finding three new major concentrations of petroglyphs. These discoveries would lead him to publish several important volumes on the prehistory of the Eastern Desert and the interpretation of its rock art. Just two years after Resch's travels through the deserts of Upper Egypt, the imminent construction of the High Dam at Aswan forced a change in archaeologists' priorities. The United Nations organization UNESCO was mobilized to coordinate international efforts aimed at recording the archaeology of Nubia (the Nile Valley south of Aswan), before it was lost forever beneath the rising waters of Lake Nasser. Archaeological missions from more than a dozen countries took part. Perhaps the most famous outcome of this unprecedented international cooperation was the dismantling and re-erection of the great temples of Ramesses II at Abu Simbel. However, away from the spotlight of publicity, other work of equal importance was being done.

Expeditions to record the rock art of Nubia (as opposed to Egypt) had already taken place some decades earlier. In the 1920s, that golden age of Egyptological discovery when Howard Carter and Lord Carnarvon stumbled upon the tomb of Tutankhamun in the Valley of the Kings, the great desert explorer Leo Frobenius led an expedition to the Lower Nubian part of the Eastern Desert. During the course of several weeks in 1927, he recorded a large number of rock art sites south of the Red Sea port of Berenike. He was already familiar with prehistoric petroglyphs, having observed and recorded numerous sites further north: near Aswan, in the Wadi Hellal behind Elkab, in the Wadi Miya, and along the Wadi Barramiya near Kanais. A short time later, over a period of ten years from 1929 to the outbreak of the Second

World War, the English antiquary J. H. Dunbar conducted no fewer than twenty-five separate 'petroglyphic surveys' along the Lower Nubian Nile Valley, from the First to the Second Cataracts. Each survey lasted for between four and ten days, and the results were spectacular. At sites on both sides of the river, Dunbar recorded a wealth of rock art, ranging in date from prehistoric to modern times. As he himself commented, 'wherever there are suitable rocks, whether on the east or on the west, there are the rock-pictures also'.

Given the excellent results of these early forays into Nubia, it is not surprising that some of the archaeologists working in the area twenty-five years later under the auspices of UNESCO should have targeted rock art as their main focus of research. During two seasons in 1963 and 1964, a Czechoslovak expedition led by Professor Zbyněk Žába spent a total of three months locating and recording petroglyphs on the cliffs either side of the Nile, in much the same area that Dunbar had explored. The west bank was surveyed rather more intensively than the east, and the archaeologists did not venture very deep into the desert. Nevertheless, the Žába expeditions brought to light many thousands more petroglyphs, again ranging in date from prehistoric to pharaonic times. Had the world's eyes not been fixed on the stone temples of Nubia and the remarkable salvage operation taking place at Abu Simbel, Žába's work might have received greater attention. Curiously, as with Winkler's discoveries twenty-five years earlier, fate cruelly intervened to prevent proper appreciation of the Czechoslovak results. In 1971, as he was still working on the final survey report, Žába died. A preliminary volume of results (entitled *The Rock Inscriptions of Lower Nubia*) was published posthumously three years later, together with a companion study (*Some Nubian Petroglyphs*) by Žába's colleague Miroslav Verner. Perhaps because of the international situation, both in the Middle East and in Europe – where Czechoslovakia now found itself in the grip of a hard-line Communist regime, its academics relatively isolated from Western scholarship – these important publications received comparatively little comment. The expedition's publication efforts were dealt a further blow that same year, 1974, with

the untimely death of František Váhala, chief editor of the full petroglyph catalogue. Only in 1999 did the catalogue finally see the light of
day, thanks to the efforts of Váhala's pupil Pavel Červíček. At last, the
results of those Czechoslovak surveys in the 1960s are available to an
international readership, at a time when the study of petroglyphs is more
popular than ever before. If Winkler's time has come, so too has Žába's.

The work and fortunes of the two men are linked in another way as
well. From the early 1970s, surrounded by colleagues who had partici-
pated in the Czechoslovak survey of Nubia, the young Egyptologist
Červíček became fascinated by the subject of rock art. His interest was
drawn at first to the results of a German expedition that had travelled
through the Libyan desert in the 1920s, recording the numerous rock
engravings and paintings in the region. A little later, Červíček turned
his attention to Winkler's work. The Czech scholar soon realized that
Winkler's two preliminary volumes contained only a fraction of the
petroglyphs that had been found during his two long seasons in the
desert. So Červíček set out to publish the rest of Winkler's extraordinary discoveries and bring him the credit he was due. By now working
in Germany, Červíček had the inspired idea of trawling through
Winkler's surviving papers and notebooks in the company of the
person still alive who knew the explorer best: his second wife Hedwig
Maria. The result of Červíček's pioneering research was published in
1986 (as *Rock Pictures of Upper Egypt and Nubia*). Unfortunately, because
of the costs at that time of publishing photographs, only a selection of
the Winkler archive could be included in the volume. None the less,
Červíček's efforts began the slow process of bringing Winkler's work to
the wider audience it deserved.

At the very same time, also in Germany, the Egyptologist Gerard
Fuchs was beginning his studies of north African rock art. For him,
there was only one way to advance the subject: a new expedition into
the Egyptian desert in search of petroglyphs. Access to the remoter
parts of the country was still difficult in the 1980s, with large areas of
the Eastern Desert under military control and therefore out of bounds
to visitors. The most accessible area lay along the Wadi Barramiya,

which provides the route for the main road linking Edfu in the southern Nile Valley to Mersa Alam on the Red Sea coast. Fuchs knew that Resch, and Weigall before him, had found dense concentrations of rock art in this wadi, and there were good prospects of further discoveries. Fuchs was not to be disappointed. His surveys in the Wadi Barramiya and the adjoining Wadi Miya brought to light half a dozen new rock art sites. Perhaps more importantly, they opened the eyes of Egyptologists once more to the Eastern Desert: its relative accessibility, at least in parts; and its great potential for significant new discoveries.

The same had been true of two small-scale American expeditions in the mid- and late-1980s. In 1984, husband and wife team Donald and Susan Redford conducted a preliminary survey along the Wadi Hammamat, confining themselves to sites that were relatively accessible from the main road. Unlike Weigall and Winkler, they depended on motor transport rather than go-anywhere camels. Their results were encouraging enough to prompt them to return again in June 1986. This time, they made detailed recordings of the petroglyphs and hieroglyphic inscriptions encountered along a 12-kilometre stretch of the wadi, from Qusur el-Banat (Winkler's Site 1) in the west to the edge of the Black Mountains in the east. Although their drawings and photographs remain useful, an inadequate knowledge of prehistoric Egyptian culture led the Redfords to make numerous errors when they attempted to date the petroglyphs. As we shall see in the next chapter, it is possible to date much of the Eastern Desert rock art, but it requires real familiarity with the prehistoric archaeological material from the Nile Valley. The year after the Redfords' second desert trip, another American duo, Sharon Herbert and Henry Wright, led their own survey of virtually the same area. However, they were not looking for petroglyphs but for other archaeological remains of human activity – which they found in abundance. Desert archaeology had truly developed a new momentum. It was feeding off a more general interest in the formative periods of ancient Egyptian civilization. This had been growing since the 1970s, largely thanks to a number of excavations at key sites in the Nile Valley. Hence the ground was prepared; and the fieldwork of the 1980s, building on Červíček's careful library-based studies, planted a seed that was to sprout, grow and flourish in the most remarkable way.

The saying 'What goes around comes around' is certainly applicable to theories about ancient Egypt. All too often, old, forgotten hypotheses are resurrected by writers searching for a new angle on the civilization of the pharaohs. For example, as early as the 1880s, the 'father of Egyptian archaeology' Flinders Petrie noted the importance of stars, and of stellar alignment, in the construction of the Great Pyramid at Giza. A century later, fringe writers revisited Petrie's observations, cashing in on the New Age fascination with cosmology. The resulting torrent of speculative books on the pyramids and their significance has been a publishing phenomenon. It has also, in many ways, redefined the relationship between Egyptology as a science and a mass-market lay audience. Scarcely surprising then, that the once-popular 'master race' theory – which had been weakened, if not quite overturned, by subsequent scholarship – should find itself ripe for resurrection at the end of the twentieth century.

After half a century of neglect, Winkler's 'Eastern Invaders' hypothesis was brought back to life in the late 1990s by historian David Rohl. His book *Legend* tried to use diverse archaeological data, supported by alternative etymologies of important ancient names, to demonstrate the historical accuracy of many Old Testament stories. A key element in the book was the theory of a 'master race' (renamed 'dynastic race' to avoid offensive political overtones), held to be responsible for founding ancient Egyptian civilization. Rohl identified these ancestors (or 'Followers of Horus', the name given by the ancient Egyptians themselves to their legendary forebears) as Mesopotamians, citing the boat petroglyphs of the Eastern Desert as important supporting evidence. Like other unorthodox writers before him, Rohl found a large and eager audience. Academics have, on the whole, been rather less enthusiastic.

Whatever the merits of his work, Rohl certainly succeeded in focussing attention, once more, on the remarkable rock art of the

Eastern Desert. While researching his book, Rohl made pioneering trips into this inaccessible region, in Winkler's footsteps; only this time, it was with the aid of good modern maps, four-wheel-drive vehicles and Global Positioning System satellite navigation. These early trips succeeded in forging a path through the wadis and sand dunes, to locations previously reached only by camel or donkey. Rohl successfully relocated many of Winkler's most important petroglyph sites, and discovered many more. Recognizing the huge appeal of the petroglyphs, and of the desert itself, Rohl teamed up with a holiday company, Ancient World Tours, to launch adventure safaris into the Eastern Desert. Each trip would be accompanied by an expedition leader, and the participants would be briefed on how to record any petroglyphs they encountered during their trip. At the end of each holiday, all the new discoveries would be collated. In time, the results would be sufficient to produce a book. In this way, Winkler's work would be continued. The rock art of the Eastern Desert would reach a wider audience than ever before. The 'Followers of Horus' expeditions and the 'Eastern Desert Survey' were born.

~ · ~ · ~

*M*y first taste of the Eastern Desert was on my twenty-third birthday. It was spring 1992, and I was travelling up the Nile, visiting as many archaeological sites as I could manage in the space of five weeks. On this particular day, I had chosen to make a pilgrimage to one of the most beautiful spots in Egypt: the cliffs of Beni Hasan in Middle Egypt with their wonderful rock-cut tombs. After gazing in awe at their intricate and multi-coloured decoration, I found myself with some hours to fill before it was time to catch the ferry and pick-up truck back to my hotel. I remembered that the Beni Hasan region held another ancient Egyptian gem, but one rarely visited by tourists. This was the small rock-cut temple built by the female king Hatshepsut in the Eighteenth Dynasty. Now called Speos Artemidos, it lay in a remote wadi to the south of Beni Hasan. With little to guide me other than an insatiable curiosity, I decided to set out in search of Hatshepsut's temple. Following the edge of the cliffs southwards, I soon found myself out of sight and sound of the tourists at Beni Hasan. Before very long, the cliff edge became impassable and I had to strike eastwards, away from the Nile Valley, into the High Desert. I had never experienced anything like it. All around was dry rock, sand – and silence. Steep-sided wadis led off into the distance, promising more beyond. That first, brief acquaintance with the Eastern Desert implanted itself in my mind. Seven years later, it was to bear fruit in an unexpected way.

In December 1999, I took part in my first week-long expedition into the Eastern Desert. Many of my travelling companions were seasoned desert travellers. Our aim was to visit the most important of Winkler's petrolglyph sites – sites that had already been re-discovered and re-recorded by previous Eastern Desert Survey trips.

Our journey began at Luxor, teeming tourist city by the banks of the Nile. Arriving on the late evening direct flight from London, the hot night air hit me as I descended the aeroplane steps. A few seconds later, and I was hit just as powerfully by a different force, modern Egyptian culture: that wonderfully chaotic and vital press of people that sweeps the traveller up and along from the moment of arrival in Egypt. Negotiating the crowds in the terminal building, the visa-stamp sellers' booths, passport control, the baggage carousel – with its hyperactive attendants, ever eager to help locate someone else's luggage – and finally the customs desk, I fought my way through the taxi-touts and porters to the waiting coach. It came as a big relief to collapse in an air-conditioned vehicle, insulated from the general hubbub outside, and the din of honking car horns that is the unremitting sound of an Egyptian city. After a short wait for the other members of the team to negotiate the same obstacle course, we set off for our tourist hotel and a good night's sleep.

The next day gave us all a chance to acclimatize, to the Egyptian way of life as much as the weather: a chance to switch our attitudes and expectations from English to Egyptian mode. From now on, despite the best-laid plans, nobody could be entirely sure how the expedition

1 Our expedition in the Wadi Abu Mu'awwad, December 2000. The terrain of Egypt's Eastern Desert is some of the most dramatic on earth, with jagged hills, winding valleys, broad plains and spectacular rock formations.

2 The present-day inhabitants of the Eastern Desert. Three generations of a Bedouin family eke out an existence, a simple portable hut of mats and animal skins providing the only shelter from the intense sun and heat. This traditional way of life is increasingly rare in modern Egypt.

3 A secluded rock art site in the Wadi Mineh. Our expedition was the first to re-discover this site since Hans Winkler passed by in the 1930s.

4 Petroglyphs of two giraffes in the Wadi Mineh, still showing traces of Winkler's chalk. During his expedition into the Eastern Desert in the 1930s, the explorer Hans Winkler used chalk to highlight petroglyphs for photography. The chalk has survived in this site for over 60 years, because of the sheltered location.

5 Petroglyphs of humans and animals in the Wadi Barramiya. Beautifully executed scenes like this depict the very people who made the rock art and sowed the seeds of pharaonic Egypt.

6 Hunting scene, Wadi Barramiya. This complex tableau shows a group of hunters, armed with bows and arrows and accompanied by a pack of hunting-dogs, pursuing the animals of the prehistoric eastern savannah. Such scenes, common in the Eastern Desert rock art, emphasize the importance of hunting at this early period of Egyptian civilization.

7 A long-horned cow and a goat grazing for fodder: petroglyphs in the Wadi Umm Salam. This scene illustrates the reason why prehistoric Egyptians spent several months each year in the eastern savannah: to find new pasturage for their livestock.

8 Two hunters and their dog trap an ibex: petroglyphs in the Wadi Abu Wasil. Scenes of hunting are common in the Eastern Desert. They document an ancient way of life, but also hold a deeper spiritual meaning.

9 Petroglyph of boat and star in the Wadi Hammamat. This beautifully executed scene foreshadows classic ancient Egyptian motifs of the afterlife journey, such as those carved in royal tombs in the Valley of the Kings, thousands of years later.

10 A group of skirted women: petroglyphs in the Wadi el-Atwani. This enigmatic scene, on the back of a large boulder, has striking similarities to a recently excavated pot from the Nile Valley. It provides an important clue about the date of the Eastern Desert rock art.

11 Winkler's Site 26 in the Wadi Abu Wasil. Lit by the morning sun, this prominent rock face is decorated with one of the most impressive rock art tableaux in the entire Eastern Desert. It is easy to imagine Winkler's excitement when he first came upon the site.

12 Painted linen from Gebelein showing procession of boats. This remarkable object from the grave of a wealthy Upper Egyptian is very close in style and subject matter to the recently discovered rock art in the Wadi Umm Salam (see Plate 13).

13 Boat, Wadi Umm Salam. The shape of this craft recalls the boats on the painted linen from an early fourth millennium BC grave (Plate 12).

would go. We might encounter impassable sand dunes where once there had been desert tracks. Bureaucracy might rear its head and disrupt our carefully worked-out schedule. And then, there was always the unexpected chance discovery. Although we would be concentrating on sites that had already been discovered and recorded, there was always the possibility of coming across something entirely new. We needed to be ready.

Setting off from Luxor in the early morning, driving in convoy alongside the Nile, it was impossible not to feel excited by what lay ahead. Here, by the banks of the river, we could see the spectacular remains of ancient Egypt but also glimpses of a lifestyle that has scarcely changed since those times: mud huts, old men riding donkeys, women and children working in the fields to bring in the harvest. However, our destination was an even more remote period in Egypt's story, the dim prehistoric past when the seeds of ancient Egyptian civilization were first sown.

The dramatic site of Kanais gave me my first taste of petroglyphs. Here, hewn into the cliffside of a broad wadi, was a small rock-cut temple constructed in the reign of King Seti I to celebrate the miraculous discovery of fresh water in the desert. A well nearby marked the location of this miracle, which transformed and made slightly more bearable the arduous journey of mineworkers travelling from the Nile Valley to the gold mines of the Eastern Desert. Seti I may have made this spot his own, but he was certainly not the first visitor to Kanais. For, all around the temple, on the cliff face and the fallen boulders that lay strewn at its foot, there were rock carvings. Ancient drawings showed the animals familiar to the earliest visitors: elephants and ostriches. And then there were the boats, large and small, simple and elaborate, pecked into the rock by the dozen. This was an extraordinary revelation. I had heard and read about the ships of the desert, but now here they were, faint signals from a long-vanished world. What did they mean? Who had drawn them, and why? My fascination with the Eastern Desert rock art had been kindled, and it was to burn ever more brightly in the days and months ahead.

After Kanais, our desert pilgrimage took us along the Wadi Barramiya, today one of the main west–east routes through the desert.
Ancient peoples, too, must have used this natural highway. For at
favourable locations along the sides of the wadi, the rocks bore great
concentrations of rock art. One of the most intriguing sites was a rock
overhang, just off the southern side of the modern road. Here, an
ancient artist had pecked into the rock face the image of a long, square-
bottomed boat, with a central cabin, numerous stick-like passengers or
crew, and a large standing figure with a twin-plumed headdress, pointing over their heads (Plate 23). My fascination with the meaning of this
enigmatic image was matched, however, by concern at its long-term
survival. For, scrawled all over the image in paint, there was recent
Arabic graffiti. It was not difficult to see where this destruction came
from: lying so close to the road, the rock-shelter was a popular pulling-
off place for lorry-drivers travelling between Edfu and Mersa Alam.
Clearly, a bored driver had whiled away one of his rest breaks by
adding his own marks to the rocks. Unfortunately, modern graffiti is
rather more indiscriminate than its ancient counterpart. It is probably
only a matter of time before the ancient petroglyphs of this rock-
shelter are entirely destroyed.

Another rock art site nearby had faired much better, thanks to its
greater distance from the road. When we arrived, the images were
beautifully lit by the raking light of the afternoon sun. Central to the
tableau was another carefully carved boat. This time, the main occupant had upraised arms in a gesture found all over the Eastern Desert
(Plate 18). It was difficult to tear ourselves away from such a magnificent
scene, but the light was fading fast and we had to find a suitable camp-
site and set up our tents before sunset. Camping in the desert has its fair
share of pluses and minuses. Certainly, there are very few places on
earth where it is possible to feel so far away from the pressures of
modern life, or so close to the grandeur of the natural world. The night
sky is dark, the stars bright, and the Milky Way traces a river in the sky,
just as the ancient Egyptians saw it. But then there are the practicalities:
the need to find a relatively soft patch of ground, without too many

sharp stones, on which to pitch your tent; a more pressing need to locate a convenient rock, of sufficient height and distance from the main camp to afford some privacy for those calls of nature – especially urgent after a day in the back of a bumpy four-wheel drive! The solution for a mixed team of explorers was simple: ladies that way, gentlemen the other way. Not knowing quite what might lie behind or under a boulder was certainly a powerful disincentive to spending too long on these torch-light forays.

When camping in the desert, it is essential to find an elevated spot, above the level of the wadi floor. Rainstorms can come suddenly and without warning, and a tent pitched too close to the valley bottom could easily be deluged and washed away within minutes. However, on my first night in the Eastern Desert, it wasn't rain that turned out to have been the greatest threat to our safety. We awoke at dawn to find the tracks of huge lorries running uncomfortably close to the camp. A convoy of quarryworkers must have passed within a few feet of the tents during the night. This highlighted, once again, the threat posed by modern industrial activities: to the desert, its ancient rock art, and those who record it!

Shortly after sunrise, with tents dismantled and loaded onto the rooves of our vehicles, we broke camp and headed for the Wadi Shallul and the great outcrop of rock at its northwestern end, the Gebel Shallul. This looks completely impenetrable, but our drivers knew, as did their forebears, that there is a narrow gulley leading through the mountain. Even more importantly, in ancient times this gulley contained a vital source of fresh water, the Bir Shallul. It must have been a life-line to the early desert travellers, and we found evidence that at least one ancient Egyptian expedition had passed this way. On the cliff face next to the dried-up well, the expedition leader had pecked his name and titles in hieroglyphs. He called himself the 'overseer of the gold mountain', giving the reason for his visit to this hostile environment: the proximity of gold-bearing rocks. Even today, there are gold deposits in the eastern Wadi Barramiya, and the mines must have been an important economic resource in pharaonic times.

We encountered another reminder of the Eastern Desert's remote past on our approach to Gebel Shallul. Driving at some speed, our vehicles disturbed a small group of gazelle from their foraging, and they bounded away into the distance. It was a reminder that there is still life in the desert, even in its present-day arid state. The most unexpected confirmation of this came after lunch. Leaving Bir Shallul, we had not driven for more than half an hour when we saw an extraordinary sight: in the middle of this dry wilderness, a young woman was tending a flock of goats. The animals were scratching at the dry scrub, finding whatever edible morsels they could. Nearby, the woman's mother and baby sheltered from the extreme heat under a make-shift tent of rugs and animal skins. Here, hundreds of miles from the nearest permanent settlement, three generations of Bedouin women were passing their days while their menfolk traded far away in the Nile Valley, perhaps not to return for several weeks. Alone as we might have felt, traversing the seemingly empty wilderness, there were other people out here (Plate 2). But they were so well adapted to the harsh desert environment that they blended in almost perfectly. In fact, the most recent Egyptian government census shows that the Eastern Desert is still home to some 20,000 Bedouin. The continuity of life in this inhospitable region is remarkable. Or perhaps not. For in the Wadi Zeidun, where we headed next, the vegetation was surprisingly abundant. As well as the thorny scrub that is a feature of many wadis, the Wadi Zeidun has large trees, hinting at underground aquifers, topped up by rainfall on a reasonably regular basis. With just a small increase in average rainfall, it is not difficult to imagine this area supporting grass and the animals that eat it.

Leaving the Wadi Zeidun, we drove into the southern entrance of the Wadi Mineh, one of the principal valley systems in the central part of the Eastern Desert. Here, the ground was strewn with huge boulders, worn smooth by water action, another reminder of the region's ancient climate. At one point, the boulders formed a massive barrier, forcing us to turn back. During times of flood, these rapids must have been a spectacular sight – far removed from the dryness we saw all around. In the Eastern Desert, as one way is blocked, another opens, often with unexpected results. As we drove back out of the Wadi Mineh, a rock-shelter high above the valley floor caught our attention (Plate 3). It looked like just the sort of shady spot that might conceal petroglyphs. So it did, by the dozen; and we soon realized we had re-discovered one of Winkler's sites, unseen (expect, perhaps, by some passing Bedouin) for over sixty years. Traces of the chalk Winkler used to highlight images before photographing them were still visible (Plate 4). It was almost as if the great explorer had just left, and there was a definite feeling of connection with his pioneering work, bridging the six decades that separated his and our expeditions. That night, we pitched camp in a remarkable hollow, surrounded on all sides by hills. Just before dawn, I climbed a steep sand dune to watch the sun rise over the desert. When it came up, it flooded the land with a golden light – an experience never to be forgotten. If I hadn't already fallen in love with the Eastern Desert, I did so at that moment.

A new day, a new wadi. We set off early, bound for one of Winkler's most spectacular discoveries: Site 26 in the narrow and winding Wadi Abu Wasil. On the way, we startled a rare inhabitant of today's Eastern Desert, a Nubian ibex. Although ibex are commonly depicted in pre-historic rock art (Plate 8), they are extremely scarce today, clinging to a precarious existence in isolated pockets far away from human hunters. That encounter was a mere curtain-raiser to the treat that lay in store. After negotiating a steep sand dune and miles of rocky landscape, our convoy of vehicles finally arrived at Site 26 (Plate 11). The midday sun was already illuminating the northern face of the wadi. There, showing itself boldly in the bright light, was the most impressive of all the scenes at the site: a boat, some 6 feet (1.8 metres) long, containing five large figures, the highest two measuring some 4 feet (1.2 metres) high (Plate 19). Even after seeing it in books, I still found it deeply moving. It shouted across the millennia, exuding that same mystical power that once motivated the artist to create this powerful image. Its size, loca-tion, relationship to the myriad other petroglyphs in the immediate vicinity: all begged many questions. But our stay on that occasion was necessarily short. The afternoon was passing apace, and we needed to leave the wadi and find another camp-site before sunset.

Our journey northwestwards took us past the Roman fort of Day-damus. Here, in the centuries after the death of Cleopatra and Egypt's absorption into the Roman world, legionaries were garrisoned. Their task was to patrol the important trade routes to the port of Berenike on the Red Sea coast. A rock-shelter nearby, hidden by a massive fallen rock, evidently served as something of a 'lovers' grotto' for the soldiers. For, side-by-side with prehistoric petroglyphs and pharaonic hiero-glyphs, Greek and Roman inscriptions mentioned the love-god Eros and the various goings-on that the shelter witnessed 2,000 years ago. The complete history of the Eastern Desert is long, complex and often surprising!

To judge from his preliminary publications, one of Winkler's most impressive discoveries lay nearby. This was Site 18, apparently located in a tributary of the great Wadi Qash. The next morning we spent some hours searching in vain for Site 18. It was easy enough to find the spot indicated on Winkler's maps. But this now lay covered by a vast dune, the product of one of the periodic sand storms that sweep this region. A solitary ibex pecked into the rock seemed to suggest more beneath the sand; but we had neither the equipment nor the time to make a thorough investigation. Perhaps the site lay here, or perhaps Winkler had marked the wrong location on his map. We couldn't be sure. Subse-quent expeditions to the area have all failed to re-discover Site 18. A spectacular treat is certainly in store for whoever finally succeeds.

Abandoning our quest for the 'holy grail' of Eastern Desert rock art, we pressed on northwards, crossing the Wadi Hammamat road and entering the Wadi el-Atwani. We intended to 'pay homage' to another of Winkler's most awesome petroglyph sites, Site 15. As befits one of the most spiritually charged places in the entire Eastern Desert, it is not easy to reach. The four-wheel drive vehicles had to give up when faced by a steep embankment of boulders. Beyond this, the wadi bottom was covered with water-worn pebbles, indicating another raging torrent at some time in the past. The walk up the wadi took a full hour, in the hottest part of the day, but the destination was worth the effort. A cave high up in the rock face gave us the first indication that we had reached the right spot. Below, and to the right, hidden by a tree, was the magnificent boat that we had all come to see. Like the ship we had seen in the Wadi Barramiya at the beginning of our desert trip, the craft contained a tall standing figure at the stern, pointing westwards towards the prow, over the heads of the passengers or crew that filled the deck. Again, questions flooded my mind. The prehistoric artist was saying something profound, but what? Who made this enigmatic image, when, and why?

The final day of that, my first Eastern Desert expedition, took our group of hardy travellers back to the beginnings of rock art discovery, and some of the sites Winkler found at the start of his epic adventure in November 1936. One scene in particular made a lasting impact: another boat, with another larger-than-life occupant, but this time with arms upraised. And there, watching over the boat and seeming to guide it, a lone star (Plate 9). Was this perhaps a clue to the true meaning and significance of the Eastern Desert petroglyphs? This was not the end of my desert adventure, but merely the beginning of another journey of discovery.

~ · ~ · ~

*E*ven after such a spectacular week, visiting so many amazing rock art sites, it was clear that there were still large areas unexplored, holding the promise of even greater discoveries. I was especially fascinated by the tales told by several members of the group who had been on an earlier exploratory trip. They kept talking about one particular wadi that they had visited only very briefly. Named in Arabic the Wadi Umm Salam, they had dubbed it the 'Canyon of the Boats'. For, on the wadi's smooth rock walls, they had seen dozens of boat drawings. There hadn't been enough time to record more than a handful of these petroglyphs, but the Wadi Umm Salam was clearly a promising place for future expeditions to investigate. I resolved, there and then, to visit the Canyon of the Boats and reveal its hidden secrets.

And so, a year later, in December 2000, I found myself in the fortunate position of leading a group of dedicated volunteers on a
systematic exploration of the central Eastern Desert. We had flown
once again into Luxor, and spent the first day making final preparations
for our forthcoming desert adventure. Supplies were readied, and
permits checked. After briefing the team members on our route and
objectives, I headed for bed – and the last comfortable night's sleep for a
week. The following morning, excited and eager to get started, we
drove in our convoy of jeeps down the east bank of the Nile. After a
final refuelling stop, we turned left, away from the river and into the
desert. The cultivation and civilization lay behind us. What lay ahead of
us, no one could predict.

That first day in the desert was one of mixed fortunes. Not long
after leaving the Nile Valley, we turned off the tarmac road to search
for a lost inscription of King Djet, one of Egypt's earliest rulers. The
inscription, left by a royal expedition in about 2900 BC, had been
recorded in the late 1930s by a passing French Egyptologist. Since then,
no other Egyptologist had seen it. I was determined to try. After all, it
was one of the earliest historical records of the Egyptians' interest in
the Eastern Desert. Despite a fairly good idea of where to look, our
search ended fruitlessly after nearly an hour. It was a salutory lesson in
the challenges of the desert. Rock inscriptions and petrolyphs can
elude even the most eagle-eyed searchers if the terrain is unfamiliar or
the angle of the light unfavourable. Disappointed but not disheart-
ened, we continued on our way, further into the desert interior.
Towards lunchtime our luck changed, and we were ecstatic to re-locate
a major petroglyph site only a few hundred yards from the main road. A
huge swathe of cliff face was dotted with images of boats and animals.
These had first been recorded just ten years previously, by the German
archaeologist Gerard Fuchs. However, his brief publication had
scarcely done the site justice. Not only were there boats of different
shapes – one was adorned at the prow with a cow figurehead – but on
the back of a large, fallen boulder, invisible to the casual observer, we
spotted a whole family of ostrich, carefully pecked into the rock. Boats,

cattle, and wild animals: during the week that followed, these three themes came to dominate our new discoveries of prehistoric rock art. As we shall see, they are central to our story.

Pleased at our morning's work, we paused for lunch in the shade of the main cliff face. We had successfully re-located an important site, but we still hadn't made a new discovery of our own. Little did we know that one awaited us that very afternoon. The best-laid plans are apt to change, and nowhere more so than in the Eastern Desert. Our original intention had been to strike off to the south of the Barramiya road, to explore some narrow wadis that looked promising on the map. Unfortunately, the Eastern Desert road-repairers had done a particularly good job along the crucial stretch of road, building up steep embankments either side of the main carriageway. There was no way around them, and our drivers, confident over most terrain, did not want to risk driving down such a steep incline. Frustrated, we turned our convoy around, again and again, searching for a way through. As we made our fourth U-turn, a team member in the last vehicle happened to look up at the cliff face towering above the road. There, 40 feet above the wadi floor and illuminated by the afternoon sun, was a flotilla of boats, pecked into the rock (Plate 15). This was a major discovery: a new and important petroglyph site, just yards from the main road! Frustration turned to elation as team members jumped out of their jeeps and started recording. We could scarcely believe that the drawings had escaped the notice of previous travellers. Together, they formed one of the most striking collections of boats anywhere in the Eastern Desert. Fortune was on our side after all.

By the time we had finished recording the site, the afternoon was nearly over. We now had to rush and pitch camp before sunset – putting up tents on a sand dune isn't an easy task in the dark. Racing back westwards along the main road, we then turned off to the north and followed the broad Wadi Miya to a likely-looking area of sand dunes, providing soft ground for our tents. Stopping only to pick up some brushwood for a fire, we reached our camp-site with less than half an hour of daylight left. As we hurriedly put up our tents, the atmosphere

was one of excitement. Our first day in the desert had been more productive than we had dared hope. But this was just the beginning:
tomorrow our destination was the Wadi Umm Salam, the famous
'Canyon of the Boats'.

Shortly after sunrise the next day, we climbed into our jeeps and
drove the short distance to the mouth of the Wadi Umm Salam. Sceni-
cally, it ranks as one of the most beautiful wadis in the whole of the
Eastern Desert. It is narrow (less than a hundred yards in places), with a
flat, sandy floor and steep sides. A few trees soften the bare rocky landscape. The wadi feels secluded and sheltered. Perhaps it was our
imaginations, but it seemed to possess a special atmosphere – welcom-
ing and intriguing at the same time. Our first stop was right at the
mouth of the wadi, to look at the boats mentioned by earlier travellers.
There they were, strung out along a rocky ledge, about 10 feet (3 metres)
above the valley floor. Nearby, on the other side of the wadi, a rock
overhang provided a welcome patch of shade. Ancient people had
obviously sheltered here as well; for the adjacent rock surfaces were
pecked with the sort of scenes we had come to expect: wild animals, the
occasional boat, and a lovely drawing of a hippopotamus being harpooned. There was even a strange squiggly line which bore more than a
passing resemblance to our modern map of the area (Fig. 2). Could this
be a prehistoric map to guide the local inhabitants to the most
favourable locations for hunting? After all, at other places in the world
where prehistoric peoples created rock art, one of the main functions
of images may have been to act as reference points in the landscape: to

guide a nomadic population along traditional routes to essential resources. Might
the early inhabitants of the Eastern Desert
have gone one stage further, and created a

permanent diagram of the wadi system, to help them and future generations to navigate through this complex terrain? Could this be the world's oldest map?

Intrigued and excited, we reassembled and formed up in convoy, ready for the day's main objective: a systematic survey of the whole wadi – or as much of it as we could cover in the time available. The plan was simple: we would drive slowly along the northern side of the wadi, all eyes scouring the rock face for any sign of petroglyphs. As soon as the lead vehicle found a site, the next vehicle in the convoy would stop, and its passengers would begin recording the drawings. The process would then continue until all the team members were engaged in site recording. The lead vehicle would then scout ahead, looking for further sites to record in a second phase. In this way, we felt that we would be able to locate and record all the significant petroglyph sites without the risk of missing any.

Our survey method had been carefully chosen, but nothing could have prepared us for the sheer number of drawings we discovered in our first few hours. Indeed, after just ten minutes, all five teams of volunteers were busy recording new petroglyph sites. By lunchtime, we had found seven major new sites of rock art. And that was just on the northern side of the wadi. By the time we left the Wadi Umm Salam that afternoon, to return to camp, our day's total stood at twenty new sites. Never before had an expedition into the Eastern Desert achieved such success. In a single day we had surpassed the total number of new sites logged in a whole week by previous expeditions.

The new discoveries were not just spectacular in terms of their quantity, but also in quality. All the usual subjects were present: boats, hunting scenes and cattle. There were also images of people in strange acrobatic poses, a woman carrying a pot on her head, and an endearing

2 *The world's oldest map? This pecked design in the Wadi Umm Salam bears a striking resemblance to modern maps of the region. It may have been created by the ancient inhabitants to help them navigate through the landscape and to locate sites of ritual importance.*

family group of father, mother and child. This last scene was pecked into a boulder lying on the wadi floor, at precisely the spot where we decided to stop for lunch. It seemed as if the ancient artists themselves were speaking to us across the ages. Here, in this special place, they had left a gallery of images reflecting their lives, their hopes and fears, and their deepest beliefs. Our duty was now to record their art for posterity, to interpret it, and in this way to bring the distant past back to life.

Among so many wonderful petroglyph sites, there was one in particular that stood out that day. It remains the highlight of the expedition, both in terms of the art itself and its stunning natural location. Ironically, we discovered it only by chance. Several team members were working away, busily recording rock art on the cliff face. Although the petroglyphs were at eye level, they were faint and very difficult to make out. So, slightly frustrated but ever curious, one of the team decided to go for a wander. What he found will stay in our memories forever. Next to the smooth rock face covered with petroglyphs was a large natural gulley. It formed a gash in the north wall of the wadi and had clearly been produced by a torrent of water flowing down the cliff face in distant antiquity. The gulley itself was filled with strewn boulders, and its upper reaches were hidden by a large acacia tree growing on the valley floor. Squeezing past the tree and over the boulders, we climbed carefully up the gulley until we were out of sight of the main wadi. Suddenly, turning around, we came face to face with a huge vertical cliff, partly in shade, and partly illuminated by the sun. It was absolutely covered in petroglyphs. There were groups of ostrich, hippopotamus, gazelle and ibex. A magnificent boat with many oars dominated the left-hand side of the wall. Next to it, a god-like figure wearing twin plumes on his head held a tethered cow. And, watching over the whole composition, sentinel-like, were three enormous giraffes. Their tail hairs had been elongated to the same length as their legs, giving them an exaggerated sense of balance. The richness and variety of the images were breathtaking. They were also clearly significant in religious terms. Surely, this was one of the most important sites in the entire wadi. But there was still more to come.

Dragging ourselves away from this remarkable tableau, we continued further up the gulley. When we reached the top, we gazed in amazement. The stream that had created the fissure itself had evidently flowed as a waterfall: the rock lip of the cliff above had been worn smooth by water pouring over it. Below, the swirling cascade had carved out a huge whirlpool. This was big enough to hold our entire expedition (for the obligatory group photograph), and we nicknamed it 'the jacuzzi'. This description turned out to be not so fanciful, after all. As the sun began to swing round, a raking light fell on the ledge running around the whirlpool. It picked out faint carvings – of cattle, some of them tethered. It was not difficult to imagine that the people who made these drawings whiled away their time in this secluded, special spot. As they took refuge from the heat of the sun, perhaps refreshing themselves in the natural plunge pool, they carved images of great symbolic importance.

Who were these ancient artists? What was the meaning of their drawings? And how long ago did this extraordinary place resound to the sound of muted conversation and the peck-peck-peck of a stone stylus? In many ways the Wadi Umm Salam represents the Eastern Desert in microcosm. Its rock art raises so many questions; and it is to these that we will turn in the following chapters.

THE SANDS OF TIME
Dating the Rock Art

*T*he rock art of the Eastern Desert speaks to us across the centuries. To understand the people who created it and their reasons for doing so, we have to determine first just how old it is. That is not an easy task. It is rather like making a rope: individual threads of evidence must be collected and twined together to produce a strong and coherent answer.

Until the middle of the twentieth century, archaeologists were largely in the dark when it came to assigning absolute dates (in other words, dates BC or AD) to ancient remains. By observing changes in styles (like an art historian), and helped by a large dose of their own intuition, they were generally able to come up with relative dates: this object older or younger than this other object. Only in cases where an object was inscribed with text were archaeologists confident of dating it to a particular century or decade. A few ambitious scholars attempted to reckon backwards from securely dated remains to earlier, uninscribed material; but, not surprisingly, some spectacular mistakes were made. For example, in the early years of Egyptian archaeology, Flinders Petrie estimated that the First Dynasty had begun in 4650 BC, some 1,500 years earlier than we now know to have been the case. When it came to prehistoric remains, his estimate was even wider of the mark:

he dated the earliest prehistoric graves from his excavations to 7000 BC, 3,000 years too early!

The great leap forward came in the 1950s. After the Second World War, major advances in science, especially physics and chemistry, led to the development of a dating technique that, for the first time, did not rely on the vagaries of human intuition and guesswork, but on objective scientific data. It was called radiocarbon dating, and could be applied to any ancient object that contained at least some organic material. Although there are still some problems with the technique, it has nevertheless revolutionized archaeology. It allows uninscribed and prehistoric remains to be dated with a degree of accuracy previous generations of archaeologists could only dream of: a margin of error as little as a hundred years for a sample 5,000 years old. Yet, radiocarbon dating is of limited use when it comes to rock art. In a few parts of the world, such as Texas, it has been used successfully; but this is generally only successful where the art is painted on the rock (so-called pictographs) rather than incised into the rock (petroglyphs), and where the original paint included some organic substance, for example charcoal, or a vegetable resin used to bind the mixture. However, very often, any organic component that was once present in the paint has long since decayed and disappeared, making radiocarbon dating impossible. Archaeological scientists have therefore come up with a radical new technique, still in its infancy but offering great potential in the years ahead. It involves radiocarbon-dating the 'skin' or crust that develops, over long periods of time, on the surface of the rock, covering the rock art. During their slow accumulation, these crusts trap salts and other mineral compounds that can – with difficulty – be analysed and dated. So far, this novel method has been tested most effectively in Arnhem Land, northern Australia; even there, it remains a controversial and, as yet, unreliable method, since we still do not fully understand the rate at which crusts form on different rock surfaces in different locations and environmental conditions.

Help may be at hand from an entirely different branch of science. Every archaeological problem is also a scientific challenge. The problem of obtaining an absolute date for carved petroglyphs might seem insurmountable, but there is hope even here. In 2001, a breakthrough was announced by researchers studying rock art in northwestern Australia. After thirty-three years of trying, scientists finally devised a method to date the rock art in the Pilbara region. It is called microerosion analysis, and involves the microscopic examination of the rock surface. The rate of weathering for the area was first calculated by examining rock surfaces of known age – in this case eight historical inscriptions. By measuring the weathering of the rock surfaces where petroglyphs had been carved, researchers were then able to estimate the length of time since the petroglyphs themselves were made (in other words, the length of time since the original rock surface was removed to create the art). The development of microerosion analysis opens up very exciting possibilities for rock art in other parts of the world where prehistoric images occur side-by-side with historically datable inscriptions – for example, Egypt's Eastern Desert, where Arab, Bedouin and Coptic graffiti are often found juxtaposed with prehistoric scenes. We can only hope that, in the future, archaeologists will have the time and resources to study the Egyptian rock art as intensively as its counterpart in northern Australia.

For now, however, we have to rely on the Eastern Desert petroglyphs themselves for clues about their age. The archaeologists who studied Egyptian rock art in the early part of the twentieth century thought they could use the colour of the petroglyphs as a reliable guide to their relative age. This may sound strange. After all, if they are simply pecked or carved into the rock surface, how can they have a 'colour'? The answer is something called 'patination'. Just as a new stone building changes colour over time as it acquires the 'patina of age', so does the fresh rock that is exposed when a petroglyph is pecked into the surface. As a very general rule, the darker the petroglyph, the older it is, since it has had longer to acquire more of a patina. For this reason, archaeologists used to set great store by the degree of patination exhibited by individual rock art images. J. H. Dunbar certainly relied on the technique for dating the petroglyphs he found in Nubia in the 1930s.

Unfortunately, the use of patination as a dating method is not quite as straightforward as Dunbar imagined. Even on a single slab or rock, the underlying mineral composition may vary, giving rise to a variety of surface colours. Hence, even petroglyphs created at the same time on the same patch of rock may start off with different colours, and this will affect their appearance as they acquire a patina. Another factor is the extent to which a particular rock surface is exposed to the elements: rain, wind and especially sunlight. There was a dramatic illustration of this in the Wadi Umm Salam. High up on the cliff face forming the wadi's southern wall, we found a delightful scene comprising a line of ibex, drawn nose to tail. Although clearly part of the same composition, half of the animals were darkly patinated, while the other half were much lighter. At first, we could not understand this difference, until we noticed that the overhanging rock ledge caused half of the rock surface to remain in shade throughout the day. The other half was exposed to the full glare of the sun. This explained the difference in patination between the two halves of the same scene. This was a cautionary lesson: it meant that patination could not be taken as a reliable indicator of age, even within a single 'canvas' of rock art. The differences between petroglyph sites are even greater, and this effectively rules out patination as a means of dating the rock art of the Eastern Desert.

Winkler himself suggested a different dating method: he thought that the location of a particular petroglyph on a rock surface could be used as a guide to its relative age. He argued that the first artist to come along and use a rock would have chosen the smoothest, most easily accessible and most prominent area for creating his images. Later artists, if they wished to use the same boulder or cliff face, would have had to make do with inferior areas that were also harder to reach. Although this is an attractive theory that seems to make good common sense, it does not always hold true in the Eastern Desert. At some sites, groups of petroglyphs that are undoubtedly early may nevertheless be present in curiously inaccessible locations, almost hidden from view; whereas later Bedouin images may appear much more prominent. In any case, Winkler's theory would only be useful for determining the relative age of petroglyphs at the same site. It would have nothing to say about the absolute age of the images.

In very much the same vein as Winkler, the American archaeologist Whitney Davis put forward an ambitious theory in the late 1970s. It was based on his study of the rock art recorded by the Joint Scandinavian Expedition to Sudanese Nubia (part of the UNESCO-sponsored rescue archaeology in the 1960s). Davis suggested that earlier rock art generally occupied small, smooth surfaces, while later rock art tended to be found on larger, rougher surfaces. More ambitious still, he argued that petroglyphs in Egypt and Nubia could be dated by their elevation, in other words their height above the modern ground level. According to Davis, more heavily patinated, and therefore older, petroglyphs were generally found higher up a cliff face, while more recent, lightly pati- nated scenes tended to occur lower down, closer to the wadi floor. Davis explained this by reasoning that the ground level had become steadily lower over time. So confident was he of his new method, he declared that 'prospects for a final and comprehensive dating of Nile Valley prehistoric rock drawings are very good'. Alas, Davis's predic- tion turned out to be rather premature. Only fifteen years later, Donald and Susan Redford cast grave doubt on Davis's elevation theory. They pointed to the extraordinary height above ground level of some of the pharaonic inscriptions in the Wadi Hammamat. Conversely, as our own expedition discovered, some of the earliest inscriptions in the Wadi Umm Salam are found extremely close to the wadi floor. Indeed, some are even partially obscured by recent accumulations of sand and gravel.

If position and elevation are not consistent and reliable indications of age, are there any other clues for dating rock art? In their own work along the Wadi Hammamat, the Redfords used a number of different

3 *Elephant, Kanais. Petroglyphs of now-vanished animals like this prove that what is now desert was once grassland, able to support herds of game.*

criteria for assessing the date of individual petroglyphs. These included patination but also technique: to judge from other criteria (such as subject and style), it seems to be the case that in the Eastern Desert pecked petroglyphs are generally earlier than carved ones. Once again, however, this method only really helps to determine the relative age of different motifs, not their absolute date. So the Redfords looked for other clues, such as the presence of particular cultural motifs. For example, the horse saddle was not introduced until the Arab conquest of Egypt; so any petroglyph of a horse with a saddle can be confidently dated to the seventh century AD or later. Indeed, the subject matter of the petroglyphs themselves seemed to offer the most promising line of enquiry.

One of the most striking features of the Eastern Desert rock art is the preponderance of fauna that are no longer found in this part of North Africa (Fig. 3). Elephant, giraffe, even the occasional hyena: we associate these animals with the grasslands of East Africa, places like the Serengeti and Masai Mara; not with the desolate landscape of the Egyptian Desert. Could it be that, long ago, what is now desert was once also grassland, able to support large herds of game and the animals that preyed on it? Even today, the Eastern Desert is not entirely lifeless. A few Nubian ibex still cling to a precarious existence, foraging among the thorny bushes and trees that grow in some wadis. Gazelle are a relatively common sight, springing away at great speed when disturbed by a convoy of jeeps appearing from nowhere. There are also colonies of rock hyrax and flocks of birds in the desert. All this life survives in a punishing and dry environment. How much more teeming the desert must have been 6,000 years ago, before the rain belt moved southwards. Actually, it would not take a big increase in annual average rainfall to turn parts of the

Eastern Desert back into grassland. Although areas like the Wadi Umm Salam are now very dry, with only the occasional tree, other valleys are quite heavily vegetated. The floor of the Wadi Abu Wasil is covered with a dense mat of thorny scrub; near its mouth, desert gourds grow in abundance. The broad expanse of the Wadi Zeidun is even greener, with large numbers of trees and bushes. There are still occasional rainstorms in the Eastern Desert, and it would not take too many more to enable grasses to thrive year-round. Was this the case in the past, and if so, when?

Here, recent scientific research into climate change is very helpful. We hear a great deal in the news about short-term climate change, caused by the release of so-called 'greenhouse gases' into the atmosphere. What is less often discussed is the long-term change in world climate that has taken place since the world began and will continue until the world ends. These much slower – but in many ways more dramatic – fluctuations in temperature and humidity have caused a succession of Ice Ages interspersed with warmer periods. Luckily for us, we are in one of these warmer periods at the moment. Even within these broad phases, there are equally important changes in humidity, caused by the shifting of rainfall belts. Studies of rocks and sediments in North Africa have revealed a surprising fact: the Sahara desert is not the permanent feature we once thought: far from it. It turns out that the Sahara has alternated between wetter and drier phases over the last 10,000 to 20,000 years. The current dry phase only began in earnest 4,500 years ago. Before that, for a period of some 3,500 years, what is now desert received enough rainfall to support animal and human life, at least on a seasonal basis. Only when the rainfall belt began to shift southwards, around 3500 BC, did the grasslands to the west and east of the Nile start to dry out, eventually giving rise to the deserts we see

4 Arab horseman, Wadi Mineh. The rocks of the Eastern Desert have been used as canvases for art over thousands of years. This example must date to the period following the Arab conquest of Egypt in the seventh century AD.

today. In other words, between about 6000 and 3500 BC, the Eastern Desert would have been the eastern savannah: humid enough to support the kinds of animals that thrive today on the East African plains – and the kinds of animals we see in the rock art.

By examining the fauna and comparing them with the known scientific data about ancient climate change, we can in this way date some of the petroglyphs to a period before 3500 BC. But what about the scenes that do not show easily identifiable animals like elephant and giraffe? This is where another technique comes into play: art history. Anyone who browses through antique shops or bric-a-brac stores will know that styles of art and craft production change over time. A teapot from the 1920s will look very different from its 1960s counterpart, even though both objects were made for the same purpose. It doesn't take a professional art historian to notice a difference in style between a portrait by Van Eyck (who died in 1441) and another by Van Dyck (who died in 1641). In the same way, the style of rock art can give us important information about its age.

Back in the 1930s, Winkler quickly realized that some petroglyphs were quite recent. Drawings of horse-riders engaging in combat (Fig. 4) clearly dated to some time after the Arab conquest of Egypt (in the seventh century AD). Pictures of camels are quite common in the rock art of the Eastern Desert, and these cannot be earlier than the introduction of the camel into Egypt in the fourth or third century BC. As we have seen, Winkler was almost certainly guided to some of the best petroglyph sites by local Bedouin. They knew the location of the rock-shelters and shady retreats that were favoured by ancient artists, because such places were still very important for the

Bedouin themselves. At such spots, prehistoric petroglyphs can be found side-by-side with camels, Bedouin inscriptions and other comparatively recent designs. In other words, the most important sites saw continuous use over hundreds and thousands of years, just like Aboriginal rock art sites in Australia. This makes an art-historical analysis even more important, as it can help to identify the main periods at which the Eastern Desert petroglyphs were made.

Even within the prehistoric era that is the focus of this book, the skills of the art historian can come into play. One of the most reliable ways of dating an object is to find a very similar object of known age. If the two are very similar indeed, the likelihood is that they will be of comparable age. (This technique is used all the time by antiques experts who, when faced with a particular object, may never have seen an exact duplicate but will probably know of close parallels.) Egyptologists are fortunate in having a large body of securely dated material for comparison: the vast number of objects, especially pottery vessels, excavated from intact graves over the last hundred years. It is through such grave goods that archaeologists have worked out the whole chronological sequence of prehistoric Egypt. By charting broad changes in the style and type of grave goods, Egyptologists have been able to divide up the centuries before the First Dynasty into a succession of phases (in just the same way as today's antiques experts talk about Art Nouveau, Art Deco and so forth). The earliest prehistoric phase from which significant numbers of objects survive is called the Badarian, after the site of el-Badari where it was first encountered. It is dated by radiocarbon and other methods to the fifth millennium (that is roughly 5000–4000) BC. The next three phases are named after the site of Nagada, near Luxor, where huge prehistoric cemeteries produced a wealth of archaeological material. Nagada I is dated to the beginning of the fourth millennium (4000–3600) BC; Nagada II spans the middle

5 A typical bowl of Petrie's C-ware. Dubbed 'white cross-lined ware' or 'C-ware' for short, this type of red polished pottery with decoration in creamy-white paint is typical of the early fourth millennium BC in southern Egypt, the so-called Nagada I culture.

of the fourth millennium (3600–3200) BC; and the short third phase, known as Nagada III, covers the last two centuries of the fourth millennium (3200–3000) BC. Together, the Badarian and Nagada I–III phases comprise what Egyptologists call the Predynastic period.

Objects from graves of the Nagada I and Nagada II periods include some that are decorated with scenes strikingly reminiscent of the Eastern Desert petroglyphs, as Winkler himself realized. The most common category of decorated funerary material is pottery; but a rare painted linen cloth has survived from one Predynastic grave, and in another tomb one whole wall was covered with plaster, painted with an elaborate series of scenes. The trick is to match up some of these securely-dated, decorated objects from graves with similar motifs in the Eastern Desert rock art.

One of the most characteristic types of pottery from the Nagada I period has a red, polished exterior decorated with designs in a creamy-white paint. Often, the painted motifs are filled with cross-hatching (Fig. 5). For this reason, Flinders Petrie – who first classified Predynastic pottery – termed it 'white Cross-lined ware', or C-ware for short. It remains one of the best markers of the Nagada I period, since it did not remain in use in the following Nagada II phase.

However, even in its heyday, C-ware was by no means common. Its careful manufacture and finish suggest that it was highly valued. Vessels of this kind would have been prestigious objects, reflecting the status of their owner, just as a Wedgwood vase does today. The motifs painted on C-ware vessels are therefore likely to have been especially significant to their makers and owners, reflecting their deepest beliefs and experiences.

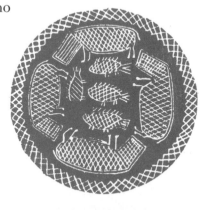

Interestingly for our purposes, these motifs are often very similar to those found in the rock art of the Eastern Desert. On the pottery, too, animal scenes predominate, with gazelle, crocodile and hippopotamus being the most popular subjects. A favourite decorative scheme for open bowls is a group of hippos, chasing each others' tails around a central point which may represent a water-lily or a water-hole. In such designs we see not only the prehistoric Egyptians' fascination with the natural world, but also their sense of humour. With their lumbering bulk and diminutive ears, hippos seem to have inspired wry amusement among the artists who drew them. However, to African people, hippos are not always figures of fun: they are dangerous wild animals that pose a real threat to humans. Even today, more tourists in Africa are killed by hippos than by any other animal. The Egyptians were well aware of the danger posed by these great beasts, and sought to control the threat they posed by magical means. Hence, a frequent motif on C-ware vessels shows a hippo being harpooned by a hunter. The harpoon is usually shown with the attached rope still partially coiled, as it lodges in the body of the unfortunate animal. A bowl decorated with just such a design was excavated in the early years of the twentieth century from a grave at the Predynastic cemetery of Mahasna in Upper Egypt. The very same motif, uncannily similar in style, occurs pecked into the rock in the Wadi Barramiya. The stylistic parallels between the two examples are so close as to leave no doubt that they must also be contemporary (Fig. 6). Here, then, we have a securely-dated comparison for at least one element of the rock art

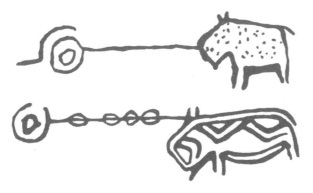

at one site. The date of the Mahasna bowl is set at about 4000 BC (the Nagada I period), and the Wadi Barramiya petroglyph must be of the same vintage. Another C-ware bowl decorated with a scene of hippo hunting was excavated in the 1930s, at almost exactly the same time that Winkler was exploring the deserts in search of petroglyphs. This second bowl comes from a grave in the Predynastic cemetery at Mostagedda in the middle part of the Nile Valley. The burial is securely datable, by its other contents, to the Nagada I period, supporting the evidence from Mahasna.

Hunting the hippopotamus was a highly symbolic activity. In later, pharaonic times, it became a metaphor for the subjugation of the forces of disorder, and the hippo became closely associated with Seth, 'god of confusion'. Even as early as the First Dynasty (c. 2950 BC), hunting the hippo was a royal ritual, undertaken by the king to assert his role as champion of created order, and no doubt to demonstrate his power and strength. (An interesting parallel is the coronation ritual of Swazi kings in southern Africa, whereby the new monarch has to wrestle to death a black bull.) Hippo hunting may already have had royal connotations in prehistoric times, since it appears as one of the motifs on a unique painted linen cloth from a Nagada I grave at Gebelein. As we shall see in Chapter 5, many of the scenes in the Eastern Desert rock art – like their counterparts on C-ware pots – can be interpreted at a symbolic level, instead of (or in addition to) records of actual activities.

More prosaic than the scenes of hippopotamus hunting is the decoration of a C-ware bowl in the Moscow Museum. It shows a hunter holding a bow in one hand, and in the other four hunting-dogs on leashes (Fig. 7). The hunter with his pack of hounds is also a common motif in Eastern Desert rock art. There are good examples in the Wadi Barramiya and Wadi Abu Wasil (Plate 6). Further C-ware pots, from

6 *Harpooning the hippopotamus: a petroglyph in the Wadi Barramiya (top) and the same motif on a C-ware bowl (bottom). Such close parallels between rock art and securely dated objects from the Nile Valley help to date the Eastern Desert petroglyphs.*

the extensive prehistoric cemeteries of Nagada, bear similar scenes of hunting. A vase features long-horned sheep being worried by a pack of hunting dogs with bags round their necks in the characteristic fashion of Nagada I ceramic art (Fig. 8). Another vessel, this time a bowl, shows a pack of four hunting-dogs attacking a horned animal (Fig. 9). The similarities in subject, style and composition of these bowls to the Eastern Desert rock art is striking. There can be little doubt that both types of art belong to essentially the same tradition, and were created at the same period. One final C-ware vessel, shaped like a vase, is decorated with two giraffes, an ibex and a long-horned sheep (Fig. 10): all animals of prehistoric Egypt's dry grassland environment, and all

7 LEFT *Bowl showing hunter and dogs, Moscow Museum. The decoration of this vessel, and others of the period (Figures 8 and 9), illustrates the importance of hunting in the lives of the prehistoric Egyptians.*

8 CENTRE *Vase showing three hunting-dogs worrying a sheep.*

9 RIGHT *Bowl showing four hunting-dogs attacking their quarry.*

10 OPPOSITE *Vase showing giraffes and other animals. Although this vessel was made in the Nile Valley from alluvial clay, its decoration shows savannah animals: clear evidence that the people who lived in the floodplain also had detailed knowledge of the grassland environment to the east.*

found in the rock art of the Eastern Desert. The particular combination of giraffes and other wild animals is attested most spectacularly at
the 'jacuzzi' site in the Wadi Umm Salam. Clearly, the world of the
Eastern Desert artists and the world of the C-ware potters shared
many similarities.

The parallels extend into other aspects of the fauna that occur in
both art traditions. A remarkable C-ware bowl in the British Museum
in London is decorated with a frieze of four animals around the
outside: two cattle and two elephants. On one of the elephants, even
the tuft of hair at the end of its tail is rendered accurately. The depiction of elephants on this bowl closely mirrors examples in the Eastern
Desert, for example at Kanais and in the Wadi Abu Wasil. The same is
true of the crocodiles which decorate the inside of the bowl. Whereas
the artists of the Nagada I period drew hippos, elephants and other
mammals in side-view (their most distinctive profile), they routinely
drew crocodiles as if seen from above. The same convention is seen in
the rare examples of crocodiles from the Eastern Desert, notably those
in the Wadi el-Atwani. It is not surprising that images of crocodiles are
uncommon in the desert rock art: even in its wettest periods, the
eastern savannah never provided a suitable habitat for these riverine
reptiles. It is all the more striking, then, that the artistic conventions of
Nile Valley pottery and desert rock art are so similar. These parallels
suggest not only a comparable date for both types of art, but also a

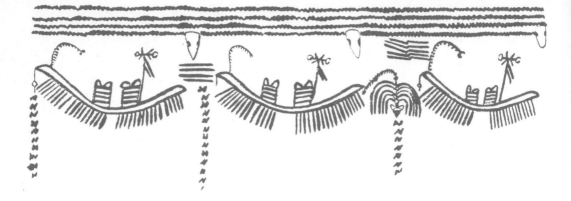

strong link between the people who worked in the two artistic traditions, as we shall see in the next chapter.

Fascinating and revealing as the petroglyphs of hunters and animals
are, it is the boats of the Eastern Desert that immediately attract attention (Plate 16). Winkler believed them to be evidence of 'Eastern
Invaders', without suggesting any particular date for them. Rohl, who
also followed the 'dynastic race' hypothesis, dated the boat petroglyphs
to the Nagada II, or later Predynastic, period. It is not difficult to see
why he arrived at this date. The decorated pottery of Nagada II (classified by Petrie as D-ware) differs from the earlier C-ware in its fabric,
technology of production, repertoire of shapes, decorative technique
(red paint on a buff-coloured background, rather than creamy-white on
red), and subject matter. The most distinctive type of decoration on D-
ware vessels shows boats, either singly or in small flotillas. These boats

11 *Frieze of boats on a typical vessel of Petrie's D-ware. Boats are a common theme on
the decorated pottery (so-called 'D-ware') of the mid- to late fourth millennium BC, but
their shape is distinctively different from the boats found in the rock art of the Eastern
Desert. This suggests that we are dealing with different artistic traditions produced at
different periods.*

12 OPPOSITE *The decoration from the Painted Tomb at Nekhen. A unique survivor
from prehistoric times, this frieze from the tomb of an Upper Egyptian ruler is
dominated by a flotilla of boats, perhaps representing a funeral procession. Similar
scenes – but with differently shaped boats – are also found in the Eastern Desert.*

are 'banana-shaped', in other words gently curved with blunt ends (Fig. 11). They often have one or more cabins, and are frequently associated with human figures in the classic posture with upraised arms. This typical decorative scheme of D-ware pottery is also found on a larger canvas: a unique painted tomb, excavated at Nekhen in southern Egypt in 1900. One long wall of the tomb was plastered and painted with a complex frieze of motifs (Fig. 12). The central, and most important element in the decoration was a procession of boats, including one painted black and distinguished from the others by its high prow. So famous is the Painted Tomb and the related D-ware pottery among Egyptologists, that anybody seeking parallels for the Eastern Desert boats would naturally think of these examples, as did Rohl.

On closer inspection, however, it turns out that the correspondence between the Nagada II boats (on pottery and in the Painted Tomb) and the Eastern Desert boat petroglyphs is very slight. Other than the obvious similarity of subject matter, there is in fact little to connect the two traditions. In particular, the banana-shape of the typical Nagada II boat is very different from the typical Eastern Desert craft which is either square with a flat bottom, or sickle-shaped with incurved ends. At only two rock art sites are there boats in the classic Nagada II style. These are at Kanais in the Wadi Barramiya, and in the Wadi Hammamat:

both routes into the Eastern Desert used throughout prehistory and history, as hieroglyphic inscriptions from virtually every period of Egyptian civilization demonstrate. We will discuss the Kanais boat again in Chapter 6. The banana-shaped boats from the Wadi Hammamat are unique in being partly painted: the only evidence to date for painted rock art in the Eastern Desert. There can be little doubt that they date to the Nagada II period; but they are far from representative of boat petroglyphs in general. The question is, therefore: are there better parallels from the Nile Valley for the Eastern Desert boats?

Fortunately, the answer is yes. Once again, we have to turn to decorated pots of C-ware from the earlier Nagada I period of Egyptian prehistory. A bowl from a grave at Mahasna is decorated with a bird's-eye view of a boat, complete with oars, what may be two cabins, and a

13 LEFT *Bowl of C-ware showing aerial view of boat. Representations of boats on pottery of the Nagada I period are comparatively rare; the few examples that have survived (see also Figure 14) provide the Nile Valley counterparts to the boats that feature so prominently in the rock art of the Eastern Desert.*

14 RIGHT *Fragment of a vessel of Nagada I date from Mostagedda, showing a boat and other motifs.*

15 OPPOSITE *Pot-mark showing a boat and gazelle. This combination of Nile Valley and savannah motifs is very reminiscent of Eastern Desert rock art. Because the pot-mark comes from an excavated archaeological context, it helps us to date stylistically similar petroglyphs.*

single human occupant at one end
(Fig. 13). This indicates that boats were
certainly part of the Nagada I artistic
repertoire; but it does not provide a very
close parallel for the desert boats, which are always shown in side-view.
Boats in profile do occur on a number of C-ware vessels, including a
bowl fragment from the cemetery at Mostagedda (Fig. 14). Even more
convincing is a vessel from the site of Nagada itself, dated to the late
Nagada I period, which bears a pot-mark in the form of a square boat
and gazelle (Fig. 15). This combination of boat and animal is very reminiscent of Eastern Desert rock art. The depiction of a square boat – a
particularly common shape among the petroglyphs of the Wadi Abu
Wasil – proves that this type of craft was also known in the Nile Valley
in the Nagada I period. This is a crucial piece of evidence for the interpretation of the rock art in general.

Both Winkler and Rohl were particularly struck by the square-
hulled boats in the desert rock art. They reminded both scholars of
similarly shaped craft: on seal-impressions from Mesopotamia; and on
the famous carved ivory knife-handle from Gebel el-Arak in Egypt.
This object has been the subject of constant discussion since its discovery in the early years of the twentieth century. The decoration
includes the figure of a ruler wearing a Mesopotamian-style turban
and holding apart two lions; and a naval battle between, on the one
hand, square-hulled boats with Mesopotamian attributes and, on the
other, 'banana-shaped' vessels of the typical Nagada II Egyptian type.
This has been interpreted as the record of a conflict between 'Eastern
Invaders' and native Egyptians in the later Predynastic period.
However, given what we know of Egyptian art (see Chapter 5), the decoration is highly unlikely to record a real event, especially one in which
the Egyptians came off worse. Nevertheless, there can be little doubt

that the knife-handle was imported from Mesopotamia or carved by a Mesopotamian craftsman in Egypt. The correspondence between the square-hulled boats on the knife-handle and those in the Eastern Desert would certainly suggest a foreign inspiration for the petroglyphs – were it not for the fact that the knife-handle is dated to *c.* 3100 BC, almost a thousand years later than the rock art. Contemporary with the Gebel el-Arak knife are the earliest images of square-hulled boats from Mesopotamia itself, which occur on seal-impressions from the city of Uruk. The presence of a square-hulled boat on a Nagada I pot from Egypt proves that the motif was part of the native Egyptian artistic repertoire long before it became popular in Mesopotamia. Winkler's argument could be turned on its head: the square-hulled boats of Mesopotamian imagery could be evidence of Egyptian inspiration, rather than the other way around. The pot-mark from Nagada not only provides an important clue to the date of the petroglyphs; it also helps to reject the 'Eastern Invaders' theory of their inspiration.

Most striking of all, in terms of providing a securely dated parallel for the Eastern Desert rock art, and especially for the boat petroglyphs, is a unique object from a grave at el-Amra in Upper Egypt. The excavations at this cemetery in 1901 produced the first evidence for the Nagada I culture, which Petrie originally named 'Amratian' in honour of the site. One of the burials, numbered a41, contained a variety of items, including eight pottery vessels, a cosmetic palette made from siltstone, and a clay doll with curly hair and a curly beard. Most curious of all was a box measuring 9 inches long by 6 inches wide (23 by 14 centimetres), made from red polished pottery. Four sides of the box were decorated with charcoal drawings (Fig. 16). One side showed a hippopotamus, similar in style to those painted on C-ware vessels and to

16 *Charcoal drawings on the sides of a pottery box. The decoration of this unique object, from a grave in the Nile Valley, is strikingly similar to the Eastern Desert rock art. The incurved sickle-shaped boat, in particular (top right, above), is closely paralleled by examples in the Wadi Barramiya.*

petroglyphs in the Eastern Desert. The drawing on the second side is more difficult to interpret, but the one on the third side is quite clear: it shows a line of six giraffes, rendered rather schematically so that their bodies look more like railings. They walk in line facing right, above a row of black triangles which may symbolize the hill country of the eastern savannah. Once again, they call to mind the giraffes from the Wadi Umm Salam. The fourth, and final decorated side of the box shows a crocodile underneath a boat. Significantly, the boat is sickle-shaped with incurved ends; it has a central cabin, and a pair of fronds or horns adorning the prow. Precisely similar boats are commonly found at rock art sites in the Wadi Barramiya (compare the upper boat on Plate 16). The correspondence between the desert petroglyphs and a box made from Nile Valley clay, interred in a grave close to the river, is uncanny – and a key piece of evidence. Grave a41 at el-Amra is clearly datable to the Nagada I period, and provides the clearest securely dated parallel for the Eastern Desert boats. How appropriate that it should come from the site which first gave its name to this extraordinarily creative period of Egyptian prehistory!

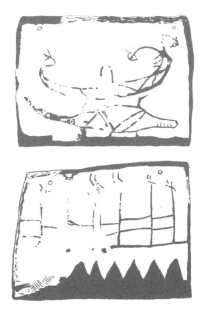

Another object from a Nagada I-period grave is a unique survivor. This is the painted linen cloth, excavated by an Italian expedition working at Gebelein, also in Upper Egypt, in the years before the First World War. The cloth had disintegrated into fragments over the millennia since it was buried with its owner. But enough still survived to give an insight into an otherwise forgotten art-form: the Predynastic craft of textile manufacture. The scenes with which the cloth is decorated recall the motifs found on C-ware pottery, including the harpooning of a hippopotamus. However, the central element of the design is a procession of boats (Plate 12). Each boat is sickle-shaped and is propelled by multiple oarsmen. The shape of the boats, the position of the oarsmen and the angle of the oars themselves are all paralleled in our remarkable discovery from the Wadi Umm Salam. On the main wall of petroglyphs leading to the spectacular 'jacuzzi' site, the composition is dominated by just such a boat (Fig. 17). When I first saw it, illuminated by the golden afternoon sun, I was reminded immediately of the Gebelein painted cloth. The similarities are indeed striking, and it provides another piece of evidence for the date of the Eastern Desert rock art.

Flashes of inspiration can often come out of the blue. While wandering through the gloomy and little-visited side-galleries of the Egyptian Museum in Cairo in 2000, I came upon a dim and dusty case full of pottery from the Nagada I period. One particular bowl, languishing in the darkest corner, immediately struck me. Its provenance is not recorded, but its fabric, finish and decoration clearly identify it as a

product of the Nagada I potters. Its
decoration is unique in bringing
together so many of the elements
commonly found on C-ware vessels –
and in Eastern Desert rock art – in a
single composition. Gazelles, a crocodile,
a hippo being harpooned, and a sickle-
shaped boat with oars: all these motifs are
arranged around the bowl in what could almost have been
an artist's trial-piece. Overlooked by generations of scholars and visitors to the Egyptian Museum, this bowl truly represents the Eastern
Desert petroglyphs in microcosm (Fig. 18). Here we seem to have proof
that the same range of decorative motifs employed by the petroglyph-
makers were very much part of the artistic repertoire of the potters
who made C-ware vessels. The case for dating the Eastern Desert rock
art to the Nagada I period looks stronger and stronger.

Of course, some of the most striking images from the desert are not
animals or even boats but human figures (Plate 5). Particularly frequent
are people (or gods – sometimes it is difficult to decide which) wearing
two projections on their head, variously identified as fronds, feathers or
horns. The figures from the Wadi Abu Wasil are thus adorned, and most
of the figures in the Wadi Umm Salam are similarly represented. The
same distinctive adornment is also seen on figures painted on an

17 OPPOSITE *Boat, Wadi Umm Salam. The shape of this craft recalls the boats on the
painted linen from an early fourth millennium BC grave (Plate 12).*

18 ABOVE *C-ware bowl dating from the Nagada I period (early fourth millennium BC),
now in the Cairo Museum. This vessel, long neglected by scholars, is a remarkable
microcosm of early prehistoric art. Its decoration brings together many of the themes
found in contemporary rock art.*

elegant C-ware vase from Upper Egypt, now in Brussels. Here, the decorator has taken care to depict the projections in great detail, and they most closely resemble fronds of foliage. The largest figure wears fronds in his hair and also carries his arms in the upraised posture so frequently found in the Eastern Desert rock art. Once again, the parallels between the decorated pottery of the Nagada I period and the petroglyphs are striking. Winkler himself recognized these similarities. One of the best parallels for his so-called 'wedge-shaped people' (see next chapter) is the decoration on a C-ware vase in London's Petrie Museum of Egyptian Archaeology. The scene shows two people with wedge-shaped torsos connected by a rope (Fig. 19). Its precise significance is elusive, but the style of human depiction exactly mirrors that seen in the Eastern Desert. Similarly, the bowl from Mahasna (mentioned above), which shows a scene of hippo hunting, bears the image of a human figure corresponding very closely to another of Winkler's stylistic groupings, his so-called 'Dirwa-people'. In the face of this compelling evidence, Winkler had no hesitation in dating much of the Eastern Desert rock art to the Nagada I period.

Some of the most spectacular Egyptological discoveries of recent years have been made at the site of Abydos. Here, on the west bank of the Nile in Upper Egypt, German archaeologists have been excavating a huge Predynastic cemetery, spanning ten centuries from

19 *Vase dating to the early fourth millennium* BC, *showing two human figures. Objects like this bring us face-to-face with the prehistoric Egyptians, the people who created the Eastern Desert rock art and sowed the seeds of pharaonic civilization.*

20 OPPOSITE *Skirted women, Wadi el-Atwani (top) and the same motif in three dimensions on a pottery vessel. This is a striking example of the close stylistic similarities between the Eastern Desert rock art and designs on Nile Valley pottery, suggesting that both were created at the same period by the same group of people.*

the Nagada I period to the First Dynasty. Towards the end of the Predynastic period, it is clear that the cemetery had become the exclusive burial-ground of the local ruling class. The graves of this period are large, brick-lined constructions with several chambers and a wealth of burial goods. Earlier, however, the Abydos cemetery seems to have been used by a much greater cross-section of the population. There are simple pits cut into the surface gravel with no more than a few pots. There are also burials which, although by no means wealthy, nevertheless hint at the sophistication and social complexity of the local community in early Predynastic times. One such grave was numbered U-502 by its excavators. The skeleton laid inside was that of a child. As we shall see in Chapter 4, the fact that people took the same time and trouble over the burial of children as they did for adults says something important about Egyptian society at this early period. Even more striking, though, than the tomb-owner's identity was one of the objects buried alongside. It is a bowl of the red-polished hand-made pottery so typical of the Nagada I period; but nothing is typical about its decoration. For around the rim stand eight women, modelled in clay and stuck to the inside of the vessel. Each figure has been given individual features; all are shown wearing white-painted skirts; and all hold hands in a ring around the top of the bowl (Fig. 20, bottom). This charming artifact is quite unique, and its survival over nearly 6,000 years is remarkable. In the same grave, a series of broken male figures probably came from a companion bowl, though the vessel itself had not survived. Was the intact bowl decorated merely a child's plaything?

I vividly remember from my own childhood a special child's breakfast bowl with rabbits running around the rim. Perhaps the bowl from Abydos tomb U-502 was the Predynastic Egyptian equivalent; or perhaps it held a deeper significance. Unless and until further examples come to light, we cannot be sure. But a petroglyph in the Wadi el-Atwani, north of the Wadi Hammamat, certainly suggests that the motif of a group of skirted women holding hands held some particular meaning in prehistoric Egypt. The petroglyph is one of the most intriguing in the whole corpus of Eastern Desert rock art. It is also one of the most difficult to record, being carved on the back of a boulder lying close to the cliff on the southern side of the wadi. The rock face is permanently shaded, and its inaccessibility further hampers photography. Yet the subject matter is not hard to discern: seven skirted women, standing in a line, holding hands (Plate 10 and Fig. 20, top). It is an exact parallel, but in two dimensions rather than three, of the bowl from Abydos tomb U-502. So precise is the correspondence between pottery vessel and petroglyph that there can be no doubt whatsoever that both were made at the same time. The excavations at Abydos have therefore provided us, qute unexpectedly, with a firm date for at least this Eastern Desert petroglyph: the Nagada I period of Predynastic Egypt, in other words 4000 BC or a little later.

Another grave in the same cemetery at Abydos produced an equally unexpected and important discovery. Tomb U-239 may well have been robbed in antiquity, for the sole surviving object was a tall vase of C-

21 ABOVE *Scene from vase showing captives and smiting. One of the most important discoveries in Egypt of recent years, this decorated pot preserves the earliest known example of what was to become the quintessential icon of Egyptian kingship: the ruler with his mace, smiting a group of bound captives.*

22 BELOW *Boat with a man holding a mace, Wadi Abu Wasil. Like the decorated vessel from Abydos (Figure 21), this rock art scene shows that the iconography of power was already being developed in the early fourth millennium BC. Such scenes mark the origins of pharaonic rule.*

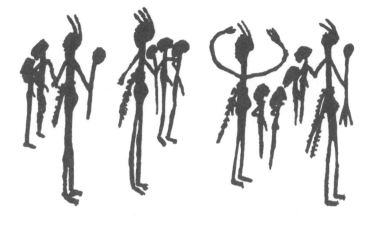

ware. A single pot it may have been, but again there was nothing ordinary about its decoration. In a complex scene which wraps around the vessel, a ruler wearing plumes in his hair and an animal tail attached to his waist-band brandishes a mace next to a group of bound captives (Fig. 21). This is the earliest known example of what was to become the quintessential motif of Egyptian authority: the king smiting his enemies. It is repeated down the centuries, from the ceremonial palette of King Narmer at the dawn of Egyptian history to the walls of Ptolemaic temples some 3,000 years later. Here it is, on a humble pot from 1,000 years before the formation of the Egyptian state. The image of the ruler with mace in hand is also found in the Eastern Desert, at one of the many remarkable rock art sites in the Wadi Abu Wasil. Here the 'mace man' stands in a boat, his superhuman stature emphasizing his exalted status (Fig. 22). Until the discovery of the Abydos vase, the earliest known example of the smiting motif came from the Painted Tomb, dating to the Nagada II period. Now, we know for certain that the ideology and imagery of political power were being actively developed at an earlier phase of Egyptian prehistory.

The imagery of power requires distinctive attire. Throughout history and across the world, rulers have identified themselves by wearing special garments and attributes, especially crowns. Ancient Egyptian kings were no exception, and in historic times wore a variety of crowns symbolizing different aspects of kingship. Perhaps the most distinctive was the so-called red crown: a squat cap with a tall, elongated back-piece from which projected a curious curled appendage. Like the image of the ruler smiting his enemies, the origins of the red

23 ABOVE LEFT *Man wearing the red crown, Wadi Qash. This intriguing petroglyph and its companion (Figure 24) provide important evidence for the origins and early development of Egyptian royal iconography. The ruler in question probably controlled a territory that encompassed part of the eastern savannah, as well as a stretch of the Nile Valley.*

24 ABOVE RIGHT *Man wearing the red crown, Wadi Qash.*

25 OPPOSITE *Sherd of pottery showing the red crown modelled in relief. This is the earliest known example of the red crown from the Nile Valley. The piece of pottery was found in a grave at Nagada, directly opposite the mouth of the Wadi Hammamat that leads to the Eastern Desert. It is tempting to speculate that the prehistoric ruler of Nagada may be the same person shown wearing the red crown in the Wadi Qash petroglyphs (Figures 23 and 24).*

crown can be traced back to the rock art of the Eastern Desert. Among the many striking petroglyphs at Winkler's famous Site 18 in the Wadi Qash are two images of figures wearing the red crown. One is dressed in a short loin cloth and penis sheath (typical of the male figures on Nagada I-period pots). He holds the crook – an object that later came to be one of the two classic attributes of kingship, akin to the sceptre in present-day monarchies. There can therefore be little doubt that he is an individual who exercised political and/or religious power over his contemporaries (Fig. 23). The other figure wearing the red crown (Fig. 24) stands at the centre of a scene showing the hunting of rhinoceros and hippopotamus. We have already noted the royal associations of the hippo hunt, and the crowned figure certainly seems to be 'controlling' the hunt in this case. He may be the same person as the crowned figure holding the crook, with the two scenes illustrating different aspects of his role, in the manner of a strip cartoon.

Once again, the best early parallel for the red crown is found on a Nagada I pot from the Nile Valley. Excavated at the site of Nagada itself, the pot was of the black-topped red-ware typical of the period, although only a fragment survives. Fortunately, it is the most important part of the whole vessel, for it carries the design of a red crown, modelled in relief (Fig. 25). Although in the historic period the red crown was associated with Lower Egypt (in other words the north of the country, especially the Nile Delta), this piece of pottery from Nagada, together with the scenes from Site 18, suggest that the crown may have

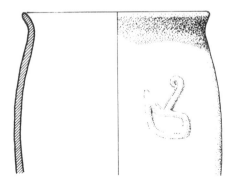

originated in the southern Nile Valley. Site 18 lies only a short distance south of the Wadi Hammamat, which itself joins the Nile Valley directly opposite the town of Nagada. It is quite likely that the figure shown wearing the red crown in the rock scene is the contemporary ruler of the Nagada region. He may well have been someone with political and/or religious power that extended beyond his own town over a wide area of Upper Egypt – including the Nile Valley and the Eastern Desert.

~ · ~ · ~

*H*arpooning the hippopotamus, crocodiles, elephants, gazelles; square-hulled and sickle-shaped boats; figures wearing fronds in their hair; a ruler figure brandishing a mace; the red crown: all these motifs are characteristic elements of the Eastern Desert rock art, and all are most closely paralleled on securely dated, excavated objects – mostly decorated pottery – from a single period of Egyptian prehistory. The art-historical evidence is overwhelming in indicating a date of Nagada I, or *c.* 4000 BC, for much of the rock art. This dating is also corroborated by a consideration of the fauna depicted in the petroglyphs. Animals like elephants and giraffe died out from Egypt following the desiccation of the eastern savannah which began no later than 3500 BC. While the tradition of rock art certainly continued for many centuries at some sites, there can be little doubt that the bulk of the early, prehistoric scenes date to the centuries around the beginning of the fourth millennium BC.

If we can now date the petroglyphs, the artistic parallels between the Nile Valley and the Eastern Desert that help us to do this also raise a fascinating question: were the same people responsible for both traditions? Unmasking the ancient artists who created the petroglyphs is the subject of the next chapter.

3

HUNTERS AND HERDERS
Unmasking the Artists

*I*t is a strange feeling, looking at images carved lovingly into a rock, and knowing that you are the first person to see them for perhaps fifty-five centuries. You feel an invisible bond with their long-dead creators. And yet the artists remain shrouded in mystery: what they looked like, where they came from, how they lived, what motivated them to leave permanent traces in the landscape. Now that we have established when much of the rock art was made, we can begin to answer the question of who made it.

As soon as he had completed his survey of the Eastern Desert in 1937, Winkler went into print in his native German with his own theory concerning the identity of the prehistoric artists. He argued that five separate groups of people were represented in the rock art. He identified these groups according to the style and subject matter of the petroglyphs, and he gave each group a suitably exotic name. Four of these names were based upon the different modes of representing humans in the rock art: Keilstil-Leute ('wedge-shaped people'); Dirwa-Leute (people with their hair in the style called Dirwa by the contemporary inhabitants of the Eastern Desert); Penistaschen-Leute ('penis-sheath people'); and Federschmuck-Leute ('feather-diadem people'). The final group – Standarten-Leute ('standard people') – he associated with the petroglyphs that show boats with standards flying from their prows. Winkler suggested that the first three groups were native cattle-herders of the eastern savannah, but that the other two groups were outsiders. He equated the 'standard people' with the later Predynastic population of the Nile Valley, and believed them to have originated in the Nile Delta. Most controversial of all, he argued that the 'feather-diadem people' were Eastern Invaders from the Persian Gulf. This theory was based entirely on the fact that human figures wearing feathers in their hair are often associated in the rock art with square-hulled boats. As we have seen, Winkler believed such boats to be of Mesopotamian origin; he did not know that, in fact, they are attested in Egypt several hundred years earlier than their first occurrence in the art of Mesopotamia! In language redolent of the Nazi ideology that was overtaking his homeland, Winkler described how the interaction between these culturally superior Eastern Invaders and the native Egyptian population had given birth to 'the People and the Empire ['das Volk und das Reich'] of the Pharaohs'.

Only twenty-five years later, his fellow German Walther Resch was to show just how erroneous Winkler's theories were. In practice, there was little to distinguish between his first three groups of people. Winkler himself had almost admitted this, accepting that his 'wedge-shaped people' also wore penis-sheaths (like the 'penis-sheath people'), and that both groups were native cattle-herders. He also had to acknowledge that people wearing feathers in their hair hardly occurred in Mesopotamian art. He had to come up with the slightly ridiculous notion that his Eastern Invaders had discovered herds of ostrich in the eastern savannah and had taken to wearing their feathers as ornaments, in a departure from their native Mesopotamian customs. Resch, on the other hand, convincingly demonstrated that the practice of wearing feathers in the hair could be attested in Egypt from Badarian times (5000–4000 BC), and was also strongly associated with the desert inhabitants of Nubia. Indeed, in later Egyptian art, Nubians are caricatured as feather-wearing tribesmen. Resch also proved the Nile Valley origin of square-hulled boats (something that had first been shown in 1942), thus demolishing the central plank of Winkler's 'Eastern Invaders' hypothesis. Another Egyptologist made the point that no petroglyphs associated with the Eastern Invaders have been found anywhere near the Red Sea coast, the supposed location where Mesopotamians reached Egypt. Moreover, Winkler later found square-hulled boats among the petroglyphs of the Western Desert! In the light of all this withering criticism, Winkler's attempts to identify the prehistoric artists were left in tatters.

Even as he was setting down his theory in print, Winkler may already, perhaps, have sensed that it was a little shaky. When he published his preliminary survey report in English a year later, his thinking had moved on significantly. Gone were the exotic names based upon hairstyles or bodily ornamentation; in their place, he devised more scientific-sounding categories for the prehistoric rock artists: Earliest Hunters; Autochthonous Mountain Dwellers; Eastern Invaders; and Early Nile Valley Dwellers. In fact, these new categories were simply a re-jigging of his earlier groups. The second category was merely a lumping together of his 'wedge-shaped people', 'Dirwa people' and 'penis-sheath people' under one heading. The Eastern Invaders were identical with his 'feather-diadem people', and he had simply renamed his 'standard people' as Early Nile Valley Dwellers. The only new feature of this four-fold division was the addition of an entirely new group, the Earliest Hunters. Once again, writing less than three decades later, Resch consigned Winkler's categories to the dustbin of history by demonstrating that a group of early hunters could not have flourished in the eastern savannah in the extremely dry period that preceded the arrival of the first cattle-herders. He also doubted that there was any ethnic difference between valley and savannah populations in prehistoric times. Winkler was totally discredited, and the identification of the rock artists seemed to have moved little further forward. Fortunately, in the forty years since Resch's study, new archaeological discoveries have transformed our understanding of the Nile Valley and adjacent areas in prehistory. We can now embark anew on a quest to unmask the ancient artists.

What is immediately clear is that the people pecking out petro-glyphs on the eastern savannah also knew about the Nile Valley. Hippos, although not common motifs, certainly occur in the rock art. Even in the wettest periods of the fifth and early fourth millennia BC, it is highly unlikely that there would have been enough rainfall to support large aquatic animals out on the savannah, so far from any per-manent watercourse. The summer rains would have turned dry, arid scrubland into fertile grazing land; and they may have resulted in flash floods in some of the deeper, narrower wadis. The huge boulders strewn about the floor of the Wadi el-Atwani and Wadi Mineh testify to the power of these floods. However, there is no evidence that parts of the eastern savannah would have been permanently under water – and hippos need permanent access to water. By contrast, the River Nile was home to significant herds of hippopotamus from prehistoric times right through to the Pyramid Age, and perhaps later. They are one of the most common animals depicted in art of the Nagada I period from the Nile Valley. They remained a popular subject for Egyptian artists right through the Old Kingdom. For example, a charming scene in the Fifth Dynasty tomb of Princess Idut at Saqqara shows a female hippo giving birth, while a crocodile lies in wait ready to seize the newborn calf as soon as it emerges from its mother's womb. This tragi-comic scene of animal life certainly illustrates the fascination of Egyptian artists for the natural world. Such scenes must have been observed by Egyptians of the period, as they crossed the Nile by boat and farmed along its banks.

So, if hippos – and indeed crocodiles – feature in the rock art of the Eastern Desert, we can be fairly certain that the artists had at least some contact with the Nile Valley. This is reinforced, of course, by one of the dominant themes in the art: boats. Ships occur in all shapes and sizes, singly, in pairs, and in great armadas (Plate 15). Some seem to show simple craft, while others are truly superhuman in scale. We will examine the significance of these 'ships of the desert' in Chapter 5. For now, it is clear that the artists must have come into contact with boats on a regular basis, for them to occur so frequently in the rock drawings.

But do the boats necessarily indicate contact with the Nile Valley? Some authors, beginning with Winkler, thought that the boats might not be river craft, but sea-going vessels. Could they perhaps represent the ships that plied the Red Sea in prehistoric times? While this theory may be attractive on one level, the hard archaeological evidence does not support it. For a start, there is no positive evidence at all that the Red Sea was frequented by shipping during the prehistoric period. Of course, early people living around its shores are likely to have developed at least rudimentary sea-worthy vessels; but when making journeys of any distance, they more probably stuck close to the shore, rather than venturing out into open water. Certainly no evidence has come to light from the Red Sea coast for any degree of activity as early as the fourth millennium BC. The earliest Egyptian port dates to some 2,000 years later. By contrast, there is clear evidence in the Nile Valley for the use of boats from earliest times: boat models from graves, and of course the boats painted on decorated pottery of the Nagada I period. It seems very likely that boats were a common sight on the River Nile in the prehistoric period, whereas they were probably still a comparative rarity on the waters of the Red Sea. Significantly, too, all the boat petroglyphs discovered so far in the Eastern Desert occur in wadis that drain into the Nile Valley. So the preponderance of boats in the rock art gives us a major clue about the identity of the artists themselves: with their knowledge of hippos, crocodiles and boats, they certainly knew about the Nile Valley and its way of life.

Interestingly, the reverse was also the case. When we look at objects found in the Nile Valley – excavated from burials cut into the gravels bordering the floodplain – we find an abundance of symbolic connections with the savannah. Decorated pottery vessels of C-ware show river life, like hippos and crocodiles, but also grassland animals such as gazelle and antelope. As we saw in the last chapter, there are bowls and vases of C-ware decorated with hunting scenes where packs of dogs attack ibex, gazelle and long-horned sheep; others featuring elephants or giraffe; and a remarkable vase which seems to show a gazelle being preyed upon by a vicious-looking hyena.

It is not only the painted decoration that demonstrates the Nile Valley dwellers' knowledge of savannah life. On many prehistoric pots, a mark of some sort was incised into the wet clay by the potter before the vessel was fired. The particular mark chosen may have signified the potter's identity, the intended contents of the pot, the geographical location where it was made, or some other aspect of production. Alternatively, a potter may simply have selected an object from his or her own experience or imagination. It is remarkable, then, that many of the pot-marks on vessels made in the Nile Valley from alluvial (river) clay should show motifs clearly associated with the dry grassland environment. A pot-mark from Nagada itself, on a vessel securely dated to the Nagada I period, shows an elephant (Fig. 26), while another shows an ibex – both animals confined to the regions bordering the Nile Valley. The pot-mark on another vessel – discussed in the last chapter – brings together emblems of savannah and river valley in the form of a gazelle and a square-hulled boat. Indeed, boats of various shapes are quite commonly found as pot-marks, together with other riverine motifs such as hippos and crocodiles. But it is striking that the people who sat by the banks of the Nile and made pottery from the rich alluvial clay knew enough about the very different environment to the east to mark their pots with examples of its distinctive animal life.

We find the same strong connection between the two regions when we look at other kinds of object, too. The people of Nagada I were very fond of bodily adornment, as reflected in their grave goods. Hair combs made from bone and ivory are common items. Many are decorated on the top with an animal, and gazelles are among the favourite subjects. These lively and graceful animals would have been common

sights out on the savannah, just as they are today; but they are unlikely to have been glimpsed on the floodplain of the Nile. Hair combs were relatively commonplace items, but the wealthiest members of Nagada I society had access to infinitely more luxurious possessions, as we can see in some of the richest graves from the period which contain a dazzling variety of unusual and exotic objects. A particularly outstanding burial at the site of Abadiya in Upper Egypt must have belonged to an important local leader (Fig. 27). Known as tomb B101, it contained the usual pottery vessels (although in unusually large numbers), together with numerous rarer items, including six strange balls of whitened clay. One is decorated with black zig-zag bands, in imitation of a protective woven bag. Whatever these objects were meant to represent was evidently both valuable and fragile. Luckily, we do not have to guess in

26 OPPOSITE *Pot-mark showing an elephant. Potters working in the Nile Valley, using clay from the river bank, nevertheless knew about the other world of prehistoric Egypt: the eastern savannah with its herds of game. The person who scratched this mark into a pot before it was fired had clearly seen an elephant, and must have spent time away from the banks of the Nile.*

27 ABOVE *Objects from tomb B101 at Abadiya. The contents of this wealthy prehistoric burial show a blend of Nile Valley and eastern savannah influences, including pots made from alluvial clay, one of which is decorated with an antelope; model ostrich eggs; and cosmetic palettes made of siltstone from the Wadi Hammamat, one of which is shaped like a hippopotamus, the classic river animal.*

this case, since their size and shape betrays their true purpose: they are imitation ostrich eggs – just as good in the afterlife as the real thing, and much less likely to get broken. Real examples are found very occasionally in graves of the same period, indicating an early fascination with these remarkable products of nature. An ostrich egg from a grave at Nagada is carved with a pair of antelope (Fig. 28), reinforcing the object's associations with the dry savannah where the ostriches themselves lived. The customs of the rich and powerful are remarkably unchanging throughout human history. Just as the aristocratic rulers of Renaissance Europe, to demonstrate their wealth and sophistication, had ostrich eggs and other curios mounted in elaborate gilt and jewelled settings, so their Egyptian counterparts some 5,500 years earlier did the same – and took their treasures (or suitable replicas) with them to the grave. If the model ostrich eggs buried in Abadiya tomb B101 reflect its owner's connections with the eastern savannah, so does the jewellery. Among the hundreds of beads found in the grave were 144 made from carnelian, a translucent red stone. Carnelian was highly prized throughout ancient Egyptian civilization, and the main source of the stone was the Eastern Desert. The beads in tomb B101 emphasize the owner's economic power: he was clearly someone who could obtain significant quantities of exotic objects from far afield.

The model ostrich eggs, carnelian beads, and a pottery vessel incised with the picture of an antelope all stress the strong links between the community of Abadiya and its savannah hinterland. But there is no doubt that the owner of tomb B101 also considered himself part of the Nile Valley and its distinctive way of life. Particularly noteworthy are the numerous grave goods connected with that denizen of

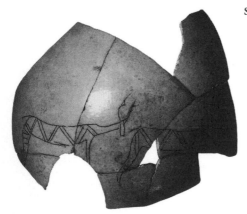

the Nile, the hippopotamus: a pair of small hippopotamus pendants carved from pink limestone; three clay hippopotamus models; nine bracelets and three combs made from hippopotamus ivory; and three complete tusks. The Predynastic ruler of Abadiya seems almost to have been obsessed by the symbolism of the hippopotamus. Perhaps we can detect that ancient association between hippo hunting and political authority that characterized Egyptian kingship at the dawn of history.

A final hippo-shaped object from tomb B101 illustrates particularly well the interconnections between the river and savannah realms in the Nagada I period. It is a flat piece of fine-grained siltstone rock, carved in the shape of a hippopotamus, the eye inlaid with shell (see Fig. 27, top left). Objects of this type, carved in a wide variety of shapes, are one of the most common and distinctive categories of prehistoric grave goods from the Nile Valley. They were used as conveniently portable surfaces on which mineral pigments could be ground up and mixed with water or resin to make eye-paint. For this reason they are called cosmetic palettes. In a few, rare cases, we have found the pebble that accompanied a palette and was actually used to grind mineral pigments. In one case, a grave-owner was buried with a palette and a small bag of raw material: galena, the lead ore used to make black eye-paint. From as early as 5000 BC until the First Dynasty some 2,000 years later, palettes were popular at all levels of society. They reflect the prehistoric Egyptians' love of ornament and display. In their myriad shapes, they also illustrate the creativity of Egyptian craftsmen. But, above all, they emphasize the strong bonds between the Red Sea hills and the Nile Valley. For the type of stone especially favoured for palettes comes from just one location: the Black Mountains of the Wadi Hammamat.

28 Fragments of an ostrich egg engraved with antelope. Found in a tomb in the Nile Valley, but decorated with grassland animals, this object demonstrates the close links that existed between valley and savannah in prehistoric times. The egg itself must have come from the grassland environment, and would have been a rare and valuable possession.

Even today, as you drive eastwards along the Hammamat road towards Quseir on the Red Sea coast, the Black Mountains suddenly rise up in front of you. Their colour contrasts strongly with the unending expanse of sand-coloured landscape all around. Because of the relative hardness of the siltstone from which the Black Mountains are composed, the wadi runs in a narrow defile through them. At the main quarry site, countless generations of expeditions left inscriptions on the rocks, honouring the kings that commanded them and Min, god of the Eastern Desert, who protected them. Today, the earliest historical inscription preserved at the quarry dates from the Old Kingdom. But people had been coming to this remote region to quarry pieces of siltstone since prehistoric times. The first cosmetic palettes are found in graves of the Badarian period (5000–4000 BC). They are usually simply carved, either oval or rectangular in shape. In the Nagada I period, the repertoire of shapes expands greatly to include lozenges, boats, and a huge range of animals: birds, domestic animals such as goats and cattle, grassland creatures like ibex and elephant, and river life like turtles and fish – and hippopotamus. No class of object better illustrates the detailed knowledge that the people of the Nagada I period possessed of both environments. No class of object emphasizes more clearly the strong links between the Nile Valley (where palettes were buried in graves) and the drier lands to the east (where the stone they were made from was quarried). Significantly, the most commonly used mineral pigments – galena (for black make-up) and malachite (a copper ore producing green make-up) – were also products of the Red Sea hills. Recent archaeological investigations have found evidence for early mining activity, dating back to prehistoric times, at seams of both ores in the Eastern Desert.

The objects that have survived from Egypt in 4000 BC present a compelling picture: of a society that knew and exploited the two very different ecosystems at their disposal. The people who were buried in the Nile Valley were no strangers to the savannah lands. And, as we have seen, the people who made the rock art of the eastern savannah carried with them vivid images of the Nile Valley. All of this begs the question: could the same people have inhabited both regions? Could the desert rock art have been made by the very people whose graves, with all their remarkable objects, have been excavated in the Nile Valley? In other words, could the petroglyphs, pots and palettes all belong to one and the same tradition?

To answer this, we will have to look again at the objects that have survived from graves: not at their decoration or material, but at their form and function. Let us consider again the amazing collection of items buried with the Predynastic leader of the Abadiya community in tomb B101. One of the model ostrich eggs was painted with black zig-zags in imitation of a woven carrier bag. This is not the only sign that portability was an important requirement for personal possessions. The hippo-shaped limestone pendants are provided with loops so they could be suspended on cords and worn around the neck. Beads, whether of carnelian or pottery, were accompanied by other items of jewellery: combs, hairpins and bracelets. All are small and can be easily carried from place to place, worn on the person. If we look again at the hippopotamus-shaped palette, and at its other, less elaborate counter-parts from this and other graves of the period, we find that each palette is provided with one or more small holes drilled into the top. Again, by threading a cord through the palette, it could be worn around the neck as an ornament – and easily carried around by its owner if circum-stances required. Personal possessions of the Nagada I period are characterized, above all, by their small size and ready portability. They suggest a lifestyle in which people moved around a great deal, where you had to be able to carry your worldly wealth with you, on your own body: in short, a rather nomadic existence.

The few settlements from this time that have been located and exca-vated in the Nile Valley tell the same story. At Hemamia in Middle Egypt, the dwellings comprised small, circular huts arranged in small groups together with communal storage facilities, and hearths for cooking and firing pottery. At Khattara in Upper Egypt, the settlement had clearly been abandoned and reoccupied several times; throughout the site archaeologists found thick deposits of animal dung. The sites of Armant, Maghara and Deir Tasa in Upper Egypt (see Map 1) showed a similar pattern of occupation. There were few, if any, traces of permanent buildings. Rather, the archaeological deposits of ash and other cultural material – the characteristic vestiges of human occupation – typically consisted of a series of thin layers, superimposed one on top of another. Each suggested a brief period of settlement, followed by a period of abandonment. Taken together, the picture seems to be one of seasonal occupation, with communities returning to their temporary settlements on a periodic basis, before leaving again some months later for pastures new. This contrasts sharply with the situation elsewhere in the Middle East at this time. Throughout the 'Fertile Crescent' of the eastern Mediterranean coast and Mesopotamia, the arrival of agriculture had brought with it an essentially sedentary existence. After all, if crops provide your main source of food, there is little need to leave your home next to the fields. Indeed, if you want to nurture and protect your livelihood, staying in one place throughout the growing season is an absolute necessity. If the Egyptians of 4000 BC were living a semi-nomadic existence, moving from place to place according to the season, they are unlikely to have relied upon agriculture for their subsistence. So how did these people live? What sort of lifestyle did they lead?

The first clue is provided by those cosmetic palettes that seem to have been such popular possessions. They hint at a love of bodily decoration, but also at something else. Across the world, societies that make particular use of face-paint have traditionally done so for important rites of passage (birth, marriage and death), and for formalized acts of aggression: warfare and hunting. It is no coincidence that many cosmetic palettes were carved in the shape of wild animals, the very animals that the Egyptians hunted: ibex, gazelle, elephant and hippopotamus. Palettes that were not animal-shaped might instead be

29 *Cosmetic palette carved with man and ostriches. The man wearing an ostrich mask may be performing a ritual designed to achieve magical power over the birds he is about to hunt. This enigmatic object emphasizes the complex relationship between the human, natural and supernatural worlds in the minds of the ancient Egyptians.*

engraved with figures of animals. For example, another rich burial at Abadiya, tomb B102, contained turtle-shaped palettes but also three lozenge-shaped examples, one of which was decorated with an elephant. From later in the Predynastic period comes a shield-shaped palette, carved on one side with a scene showing a hunter and a group of ostrich (Fig. 29). What is particularly interesting is that the hunter wears an ostrich mask. By magical means, this would have allowed him to take on some of the powers of his quarry, giving him extra success in the hunt. From the very end of the prehistoric period, the very end of the palette tradition, there is a famous ceremonial palette – perhaps never used but created for display purposes – which shows an entire hunting expedition. A line of hunters marches along the edge of the palette, towards the lion that is their target. The men carry bows and arrows and wear the tails of hunting-dogs in their belts, again to give them magical powers in the hunt (Fig. 30). In a world where the successful subjugation of wild animals depended as much on magical assistance as on hunting skills, what could be more effective than to prepare your face-paint for the hunt by grinding up pigment on an image of the very animal you hoped to catch? The popularity of palettes, then, suggests a lifestyle in which hunting played an important part.

This confirms the impression generated by the hunting scenes so lovingly rendered on the painted pottery of Nagada I: packs of hunting dogs, ibex in flight, a gazelle being worried by a hyena. Just as hunting the hippopotamus was a ritually charged and socially important activity in the Nile Valley, so hunting the animals of the savannah seems to have been central to the people living in that environment. Of course, hunting is one of the most common motifs in the Eastern Desert rock art (see Plate 6). Sites in every major wadi show the same type of scenes: hunting-dogs, often accompanied by their human

masters, bringing down ibex; a hyena stalking a gazelle. The parallels
are striking. There can be little doubt that the same people who used
palettes in preparation for the hunt and decorated their pottery
with scenes of wild animals also created rock art at the hunting sites
themselves.

So, Egypt in 4000 BC was a world in which people lived their lives as
semi-nomads. They spent part of the year in the Nile Valley, surrounded by its characteristic fauna. Hippos and crocodiles, and above
all boats: all these aspects of river life imprinted themselves on the
people's imagination as a series of powerful and resonant images. Here,
by the banks of the river, people used the abundant supplies of alluvial
clay to make pottery, which they decorated, either with scenes of river
life, or with the grassland animals from their other world. In the Nile
Valley, too, many of them would be buried, surrounded by the small,
portable items that told the tale of their wandering existence. Their
other realm, the eastern savannah, presented a dramatically different,
though no less challenging environment. People left their mark here as

30 *Hunters wearing the tails of hunting-dogs, shown on the decorated 'Hunters'
Palette' (two figures have been reversed from the original palette). An important feature
of Egyptian society from earliest times, hunting remained a ritually charged activity,
with religions connotations, throughout the course of pharaonic civilization.*

well, in the form of rock art. Once again, they mixed images from their two worlds: elephant, ostrich and giraffe were typical of the grassland fauna, while hippos and above all boats reminded them of the Nile Valley.

~ · ~ · ~

*I*f this was the pattern of life for the creators of the rock art, what drove them to divide their time between valley and savannah? Was hunting the only reason they left the banks of the Nile, or was there another imperative for seeking out the grasslands to the east? Clues come from both areas. The first, from a grave in the Nile Valley, looks innocuous enough: a broken pot, carefully mended by drilling holes through both pieces, so that they could be fixed together again with a strong twine. What is its significance? Of all the raw materials available within easy reach of the Nile, clay for making pottery is by far the most abundant, and the most readily collected. Fine, alluvial clay, ideal for pottery, can be found all along the banks of the river. Mixed with straw, sand or dung as a tempering agent, the clay can be worked into pots and fired in the simplest of kilns. It is no wonder that pottery making was one of the earliest crafts to develop in the Nile Valley. From Badarian times (*c.* 5000 BC), fine, hand-made, often decorated pottery became one of the hallmarks of ancient Egyptian civilization. Most everyday pottery was made at the household level, by individual families; but more refined wares were also produced, by specialist potters. A potter's workshop dating to the Nagada I period (*c.* 3800 BC) has even been exca-vated at the southern Egyptian site of Nekhen. If clay was so abundant, pottery so easy to make, why would anyone living in the Nile Valley go to the trouble of mending a broken pot? Why not simply throw it away and make, or acquire, a replacement? The answer must be that the pot's owner valued it particularly highly because, for some reason, circumstances meant that a replacement was not readily avail-able when the pot was broken. The accident must, therefore, have happened a considerable distance from potters' workshops and clay

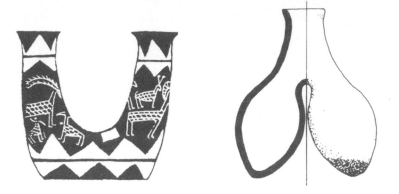

31 LEFT *Vessel in the shape of bull's horns. Objects like this illustrate the craftsmanship of prehistoric potters, and the central importance of cattle in early Egyptian culture.*

32 RIGHT *Vessel in the shape of bull's testicles. The shape of this pot acknowledges the virility and fecundity of the bull, important qualities in a society where people's livelihoods depended upon their herds of cattle.*

33 OPPOSITE *The Egyptian king wearing a bull's tail (from the palette of King Narmer, First Dynasty). This element of the royal regalia symbolized the strength, virility and fecundity of the king. There was a close association between the ruler and the bull in ancient Egypt, and cattle imagery occupied a central place in Egyptian art.*

deposits – a considerable distance from the Nile Valley. In other words, people living – and dying – in the river's floodplain around 4000 BC were also spending periods far away from the Nile; and that can only have been in the dry grasslands to the west and, especially, east of the valley. They must have had a good reason for dividing their time in this way. Surely the prospect of good hunting out on the savannah would not, on its own, have been sufficient to draw people away from the Nile and its abundant resources?

The pottery of the time holds another clue about the prehistoric Egyptians' way of life. The specialist potters of 4000 BC – who lived in the few permanent towns and practised their craft as a full-time occupation – did not only produce plain, utilitarian wares for everyday use. Like skilled craftsmen everywhere, they turned their hands to making more refined products: thin-walled drinking vessels, decorated bowls, pots in a variety of unusual shapes. Indeed, the potters of this period produced a greater diversity of exotic forms than at almost any other period of Egyptian civilization: bird-shaped jars, elegant oval platters, tall slender vases, vessels shaped like bunches of fruit. Perhaps most striking of all are the polished red pots comprising two upright cylinders joined together at the bottom by the horizontal body of the vessel, in a sort of U-shape (Fig. 31). As we shall see in a moment, their symbolism is clear: they are designed to resemble a pair of bull's horns. And this is not the only indication that cattle occupied an important place in the imagination and culture of Predynastic Egypt. For one of the other curious shapes perfected by these innovative potters was the double bag-shaped vessel, with a single opening leading to two bulbous cavities (Fig. 32). What could these represent?

Again, the answer comes from the sphere of cattle-rearing: these special pots are modelled on a pair of bull's testicles – that part of the animal's anatomy, together with its horns, that most strongly symbolizes its virility and reproductive power. In pharaonic times, the ceremonial dress of the Egyptian king included a bull's tail suspended from the belt of his kilt (Fig. 33). It symbolized the king's power and might, likened to those of the wild bull. On the ceremonial palette of Narmer, first king of the First Egyptian Dynasty, the ruler is actually shown as a

minoan ??

99

wild bull, trampling his enemies underfoot and destroying their fortified strongholds. Fifteen centuries later, the principal name of Thutmose III, warrior pharaoh of the Eighteenth Dynasty, proclaimed him as a 'strong bull'; while the famous scene on the walls of Ramesses III's temple, showing him hunting down a fierce wild bull, conveys the same impression: that the king is equal – or superior – to the wild bull, fiercest of all beasts, because he himself embodies the bull's power and strength. The pottery of prehistoric Egypt shows that, even in 4000 BC, a full thousand years before Narmer and his ceremonial palette, the imagery of the bull was central in Egyptian art and culture.

We see this also in amulets of the period. At its simplest, an amulet was a small pendant, suspended on a cord and worn around the neck to give its owner magic protection. (St Christopher pendants, worn or displayed in motor vehicles to protect the traveller, are a modern survivor of this ancient practice.) Amulets went to the heart of the Egyptians' religious beliefs, according to which evil or malign forces could be kept at bay by magical means. One of the most effective ways of achieving this protection was by wearing an amulet in the shape of something that embodied the attributes the owner wished to absorb. So, for example, a leg-shaped amulet might give its wearer fleetness or sureness of foot; a frog amulet would endow its wearer with fecundity (frogs were noted for producing tens of thousands of eggs); and an amulet in the shape of a set-square was believed to guarantee that its owner would lead a life of rectitude. Amulets of all shapes and materials were a common feature of ancient Egyptian culture until the very end of pharaonic civilization; but the earliest examples date to prehistoric times, in fact to the Nagada I period of 4000 BC. The amulets from this time are shaped like bull's heads, the horns curving inwards as if deliberately deformed to contain and harness the great beast's aggres-

34 *Amulet in the shape of a bull's head. Small objects like these were worn in the belief that they conferred magical qualities on their owner: in this case, the strength and reproductive power of the bull.*

sive power (Fig. 34). It must be significant that people chose the bull as the pre-eminent symbol that would bring them magical protection in their dangerous daily lives. It suggests that they were familiar, indeed intimate, with cattle. For the bull had found a place not only in their art, but also in their deepest beliefs.

Nowhere is this close connection between Predynastic Egyptians and cattle better demonstrated than in funerary remains. In cemeteries throughout Upper Egypt – Abadiya, Mahasna, el-Amra, Gebelein, all of them key sites for the Nagada I period – cattle were found to have been buried side-by-side with humans. In fact, there seems to have been little or no difference in the treatment accorded to human and bovine interments. At the important cemetery of Badari, in Middle Egypt (which was used for burials during the Badarian period and throughout the following millennium), bodies of cattle had been wrapped in mats, just like human corpses, and placed into shallow, oval pits, cut into the surface gravel – again, just like the graves of people. At the important site of Nekhen, the local rulers of the Nagada I period had chosen for themselves an exclusive burial ground, several miles up a wadi from the town. Among the rich graves at this spot, known to archaeologists as Site 6, burials of cattle were found intermingled with those of humans. In death, as in life, the wealthiest and most powerful members of the community wished to associate themselves with cattle. In the same way, nearly 1,000 years later, a high government official of the early First Dynasty decorated the façade of his palatial tomb (at North Saqqara, overlooking the early capital city of Memphis) with dozens of bulls' heads, individually modelled in clay but provided with real pairs of horns.

This is very striking, and it indicates that whatever bond united the early Egyptians and their herds, it was a strong, deep, and spiritual one. For the Egyptians of 4000 BC, it seems, cattle were not merely livestock to be reared and exploited: they were fellow creatures of creation, joined to humans in an intensely symbiotic relationship. This is the hallmark of a cattle-herding society, one that depends for its very livelihood on herds of domesticated animals. The welfare of people and cattle were inextricably linked. If the herds perished, so did the people. The power of the bull could give protection; but it was also thought important to show due reverence to cattle, giving carefully selected individuals the same attention in death as esteemed members of the community. Cattle *were* esteemed members of the community.

The cemetery of el-Amra, type-site for the Nagada I (or Amratian) period, provides a final, illuminating example of the role of cattle in the lives, livelihoods and culture of the Predynastic Egyptians. A few of the burials at the site clearly belonged to important and wealthy members of the local community. They were generally somewhat larger graves, and were furnished with a much greater quantity and variety of objects. Notable among the grave goods are baked pottery models of cattle (Fig. 35). These were no children's toys: the bodies buried with them belonged to adults. So we must seek a different explanation. Just as models of food and drink could magically 'come alive' in the tomb and offer sustenance to the deceased in the afterlife, so too could models of larger, living organisms. In the decorated tombs of high officials from the classic periods of pharaonic civilization – the Old, Middle and New Kingdoms – the walls are covered with scenes of offering-bearers, bakers, brewers, carpenters, metal-workers: indeed, all the personnel needed to ensure an eternal supply of food, drink and possessions for the tomb-owner if, by chance, the real versions buried with him should perish or be destroyed. Many tombs also show lively scenes of cattle, being herded together or driven through fords to find lush new pasture. Once again, the purpose of the paintings was to ensure an eternal supply of cattle for the dead tomb-owner in the next world. Why? Not for food (the other scenes described above fulfilled this purpose), but for wealth. In ancient Egypt, as in other cultures around the world, cattle were synonymous with wealth.

The census of the country's total economic resources, carried out in the king's name every two years during the Old Kingdom, was known as 'the cattle count'. Echoes of this ancient mind-set, equating cattle with wealth, have come down to us across the centuries: the Latin word for property or money (*pecunia*) derives from the word for cattle (*pecus*); our own words 'cattle' and 'chattel' are likewise from the same root. In ancient Egypt, the roots of this view stretch far back, even into prehistoric times. In 4000 BC, it seems that people measured their wealth, symbolically or practically, in cattle; and for the wealthiest members of society, it was important to maintain their economic superiority into the afterlife, by being buried with model cattle that would spring into life beyond the grave.

Cattle symbolism – especially bulls' horns – abounds on objects of the time, from hair combs to cosmetic palettes to the decoration of pottery (Fig. 36). The importance of cattle in Egyptian art and religion in the Nagada I period provides an important clue about the people's

35 *Pottery cattle model. Initially identified as a child's toy, this object from a prehistoric grave may, in fact, have served a more sophisticated purpose: magically to provide the deceased person with herds of cattle in the afterlife.*

way of life at this time. We have already seen that they were well
acquainted with the eastern savannah and its fauna; that they engaged
in hunting grassland animals on a regular basis; and that they had occasion to spend significant periods of time away from the Nile and its
resources. Could it be that cattle-herding led them to divide their time
in this way, following a semi-nomadic existence as they accompanied
their herds from pasture to pasture according to the rhythm of the
seasons? When we look again at the settlements that have been excavated from this remote period, we find not only evidence for multiple,
successive and short-lived phases of temporary human habitation; we
also encounter thick accumulations of animal droppings. This picture
strongly indicates seasonal occupation by groups of people whose
livelihoods revolved around livestock: goats, sheep and cattle. Recent
excavations in the Western Desert have shown that this pastoral type of
lifestyle was widespread in northeastern Africa during moist phases of
the climate, when there was enough rainfall to support herds of cattle –
animals that need to drink at least once a day if they are to thrive.
Towards the end of the most recent humid phase, sufficient rain to
support grazing animals fell only in the summer season. The sudden
burst of succulent new growth, throughout the wide
wadis to the east of the Nile Valley, would have
been enough to attract cattle-herders and
their livestock, especially if the pasture-
lands of the floodplain were temporarily
underwater during the annual inundation (see Chapter 4). While people and
animals were away in the eastern savannah, the rich alluvial silt that had been
washed downstream by the floodwaters
and deposited in a fine layer over the

land would bring renewed fertility to the soil. Once the waters receded again, luxuriant new growth would follow in time for the winter, and the return of the herds and herdsmen to the Nile Valley. In other words, the very climate of Egypt in 4000 BC lent itself to seasonal cattle-herding as a way of life.

So far, we have seen that the prehistoric artists who made the petro-glyphs of the Eastern Desert were well acquainted with the Nile Valley; while the people who were buried with their pots and palettes in the Nile Valley had detailed knowledge of the eastern savannah, as it still was in 4000 BC. Given these links, and the comparable knowledge of hunting displayed by both sets of people, it seems fairly certain that, in fact, they were one and the same group: small communities that spent part of their time in the Nile Valley, part in the eastern savannah. The limited settlement evidence from the valley reinforces this picture of a semi-nomadic lifestyle. The reason behind it seems to be the people's dependence on cattle, and their need to find new pastures for their livestock on a seasonal basis. For the final strand of evidence that will help to tie all these threads together, we must return to the Eastern Desert rock art itself.

At many of the sites with great concentrations of petroglyphs, such as Kanais and elsewhere in the Wadi Barramiya, the twin themes of hunting and boats predominate. But at Winkler's remarkable Site 26 in the Wadi Abu Wasil, and even more strikingly at the newly discovered rock art sites in the Wadi Umm Salam, another motif is frequently encountered: what appears to be cattle-herding. On the main rock face at Site 26, just below the extraordinary main boat with its superhuman passengers, a figure wearing twin plumes holds a cow (or bull – it is not possible to tell which) by means of a rope around its neck. A similar motif is repeated, not once but twice, on the adjacent rock face. This time, the cattle are surrounded by wild animals. Given the hunting

36 Bowl showing seven cattle. The decoration of this pottery vessel emphasizes the importance of cattle in the lives and livelihoods of the prehistoric Egyptians.

context, it is possible that these particular examples could represent, not the tethering of domesticated cattle, but instead the lassoing of wild ones. It seems highly likely that a population of wild cattle would have roamed the eastern savannah, together with the other game animals shown in the prehistoric rock art. Indeed, one of the two figures holding a cow by a rope also carries a bow in his other hand, and the animal looks as if it is straining to escape. But in the upper right of the very same scene, a man holding a long-horned cow by a rope does so with apparent ease (Fig. 37). There is no sign of straining by either man or beast; what is more, a smaller cow (perhaps a calf) stands immediately in front of the tethered one. This looks much more like a scene of cattle-herding than cattle-hunting.

The same is true of another example on the opposite side of the Wadi Abu Wasil. Here, in a rock art tableau reminiscent of a strip cartoon, a large, plumed figure appears at the right of the scene inside a

37 *Tethered cattle, Wadi Abu Wasil. There are countless depictions of cattle in the rock art of the Eastern Desert. Here, the relationship between the animals and their human masters is clearly expressed.*

38 OPPOSITE *Man and boy with tethered cow, Wadi Abu Wasil. This is one of the most important, and touching, scenes in the Eastern Desert. The close bond between the two human figures recalls the role of males in present-day cattle-herding cultures of East Africa. The elaborate head-dress worn by the cow may identify it as a ritual, even divine animal, perhaps a fore-runner of the cattle cults that were a feature of pharaonic Egypt.*

boat, and holding what appears to be a mace – in other words, an emblem of authority. To the left of the scene, the same man, in the same attire but without the mace, instead holds a docile-looking cow on a rope. With his other hand, in a touching gesture of affection, he appears to pat the head of his smaller companion, who stands behind him (Fig. 38). Interestingly, among present-day cattle-herders in the Sudan, it is the men who take responsibility for tending the herds. It is difficult not to interpret this rock art site as two symbolic scenes from the life of a powerful man, perhaps the leader of his community. In life, it seems, his wealth and influence depended upon cattle. Hence he is shown on the left (perhaps intended to be 'read' first) holding a teth-ered representative of his, no doubt extensive, herd. To the right, perhaps intended to be read second, he has been transformed into a mace-wielding figure of authority. His superhuman size and mode of transport in this second scene may indicate that he has travelled beyond the grave, into the spirit world of the hereafter. If this interpretation of the whole tableau is correct, it is particularly striking that an individual of high social status should be shown accompanied by his son. This hints at the beginnings of a crucial development for the future of ancient Egyptian civilization: the acquisition of power based upon birth rather than lifetime achievement. As we shall see in the next chapter, the discovery of rich child burials in the Nile Valley from 4000 BC points to the same phenomenon.

This process was to culminate in the domination of the entire country by a single ruling family, at the beginning of the historic First Dynasty. Here then, in the Eastern Desert, we may see the first seeds of Egyptian kingship.

To return to the theme of cattle in the rock art, in the Wadi Abu Wasil, at least, we appear to have two different types of activity depicted: hunting and herding. The two primary activities in which the prehistoric artists engaged, while out here on the savannah, are brought together in the presence of cattle. This may help to explain why cattle were so central to the beliefs and world-view of the prehistoric Egyptians. It also very much echoes the role of cattle in later Egyptian culture: where domesticated herds are emblematic of Egypt's wealth, but where, at the same time, the wild bull is hunted by the king to demonstrate his vigour as Egypt's protector and defender.

In the wider wadis to the north of the Wadi Abu Wasil there is more certain evidence in the rock art for cattle-herding. The Wadi Abu Mu'awwad is a broad, meandering valley in the same system as the Wadi Umm Salam (Plate I). Petroglyphs are comparatively few and far between in the Wadi Abu Mu'awwad, but there is one notable concentration of images, pecked into the smooth top face of a large boulder that lies on the southern side of the wadi floor. The scene, which must have been created all at one time – judging from the identical technique and patination of the individual components – shows a group of five men and cattle. Each human figure holds a cow by means of a rope around its neck (Fig. 39). There are no indications that this is a hunting

scene: there are no bows and
arrows, no hunting-dogs, no
other wild savannah animals.
Rather, it looks very much like a
scene of cattle-herding. Perhaps
each figure with his cow represents the head
of a separate family from the community that frequented this wadi.
Certainly, the immediate vicinity of the petroglyphs would have been
ideal for grazing cattle. The wadi bottom is broad and flat, and would
have provided excellent pasturage in the wetter prehistoric times. The
high cliffs either side offer ideal vantage points from which the herders
could have kept watch over their livestock. Lastly, the twists and turns
in the wadi's course mean that the upper stretches feel rather cut-off
and protected from the surrounding region – again, an ideal spot where
a community could put its herds out to graze after the summer rains.

At its mouth, the Wadi Abu Mu'awwad joins the entrance to the
Wadi Umm Salam – our famous 'Canyon of the Boats' – and it is in this
latter wadi that we find the ultimate expression of ancient cattle-
herding. Some way along the wadi there is the most definitive example
of domesticated cattle-rearing in the Eastern Desert rock art (Fig. 40).
Pecked into the side of a fallen boulder, a group of petroglyphs shows a
long-horned cow (and this time we can be sure it is a female) suckling a

39 OPPOSITE *Cattle-herders, Wadi Abu Mu'awwad. Although crudely executed, these*
petroglyphs have a prominent position on the wadi floor. They give an insight into the
lifestyle of the people who inhabited the area six thousand years ago.

40 ABOVE *Cow, suckling calf and attendant, Wadi Umm Salam. Perhaps a little later*
in date than other similar petroglyphs, this scene nevertheless captures the essence of the
inter-relationship between humans and cattle in prehistoric Egypt.

calf, while a human figure looks on, tending the animals. The scene is quite crudely executed, and it is difficult to be certain that it belongs to the same great period of rock art as the other examples we have been discussing. Whether it dates to 4000 BC or several centuries later, it nevertheless points quite clearly to the herding of cattle having taken place here in the eastern savannah, before an increasingly arid climate turned the area into the desert we see today.

The most evocative echoes of this prehistoric landscape and its way of life are found at the wadi's most haunting rock art location, the so-called 'jacuzzi' site that our expedition first discovered in December 2000. On the main rock wall facing the plunge-pool, a majestic, twin-plumed figure holds a tethered cow (Fig. 41). He seems to preside over the whole tableau, and his distinctive headgear identifies him as a god (see below, Chapter 6). Perhaps he represents the most important deity for the people who came to this site. After all, what more important role could a divine protector play than to watch over and safeguard their cattle, upon which their very livelihoods depended? These prehistoric Egyptians' concern, even obsession, with cattle is eloquently expressed by the series of petroglyphs pecked into the rock ledge surrounding the plunge pool. In earlier, wetter times, this pool is likely to have contained water after the seasonal rains. It is not difficult to imagine people sitting here, during the day, shaded by the surrounding high rock walls from the ferocity of the summer sun. As their herds grazed contentedly in the wadi below – watched over by their divine protector – the herders may have come to this

special place for pure relaxation, but they are more likely to have come for spiritual purposes. It was in locations like this that the barrier between the natural and supernatural domains was believed to be at its thinnest. Here people could commune with the spirit world, seeking help for their most powerful concerns. One way of doing this was to imprint the rocks – behind which lay the spirit world – with images of those things that occupied their thoughts. To judge from the petroglyphs around the edge of the plunge-pool, cattle occupied their thoughts above all else. For it is delicately executed, and now heavily eroded, scenes of cattle (some tethered) that decorate the rock surface. There could be no clearer expression of these ancient artists' livelihoods and identity.

The herding of cattle goes back a long, long way in northeastern Africa. It is estimated that the domestication of cattle first occurred in the Nile Valley of Lower Nubia (present-day northern Sudan), as early as 7500 BC. From there, when climatic conditions permitted, it spread into the seasonal savannahs to the east and west of the valley. By 5000 BC cattle-rearing was the most important, and widespread, form of subsistence in the territory of modern Egypt. These precious animals were not exploited for their meat – that would have been far too wasteful of a valuable resource – but for their milk and blood. Both offer renewable sources of fat and protein, and this same practice is still maintained today by the semi-nomadic cattle-herders of East Africa.

Of course, keeping cattle requires a mobile way of life. Livestock needs to move from pasture to pasture, and the herders must stay with their herds as they wander across the landscape: hence the need for objects that are readily portable, such as those that we find in Egyptian graves of the Nagada I period; hence, also, the development of cultural

41 *'Cattle protector' deity, Wadi Umm Salam. The plumed figure holding a tethered cow is clearly identified as divine by his head-dress, which remained the classic attribute of deities in Egyptian art. This petroglyph may well be the earliest known image of a god in ancient Egyptian religion.*

practices that essentially focus on the human body. Without permanent settlements, decoration and celebration tend to be expressed through the individual. This way of life helps to explain the predominance of cosmetic palettes, bracelets, beads, amulets, hair-combs and other items of personal adornment among the grave goods of the period. Far from being an impediment to developing a complex and sophisticated culture, a semi-nomadic way of life seems to have had the opposite effect in prehistoric Egypt. The widespread adoption of cattle-herding led to the dispersement of the associated cultural practices over a similarly wide area. Of course, most of our evidence for Predynastic culture comes from graves, because these have survived whereas settlements have not. Nevertheless, even though we are looking at only one aspect of ancient society – its funerary practices – it is striking that these should be so similar over a huge area. The type of grave goods and the treatment of the body show little variation from the Sudan in the south to the central stretch of the Egyptian Nile Valley in the north: a distance of some 800 miles. This would be difficult to explain if individual communities were practising agriculture with its associated sedentary existence. But if they were pastoralists, following their livestock over large swathes of territory during the course of the year, coming into regular contact with other neighbouring groups of people, this would account for one set of beliefs and practices having been so widely shared. This realization has profound implications for the origins of ancient Egypt itself, as we shall see in Chapter 6.

Unmasking the prehistoric artists of the Eastern Desert has been rather like attempting a jigsaw puzzle, with each piece of evidence fitting into place until the full picture begins to emerge. There are still many, many more pieces to go before the puzzle is finally solved; but enough is clear to begin to sketch a plausible picture of what life was like for our prehistoric artists, in the Egypt of 4000 BC. That will be our aim in the next chapter.

4

BEFORE THE PHARAOHS
Life in Predynastic Egypt

What was life like in Egypt 6,000 years ago? In order to put the rock art in its proper context, we need to understand the world of the people who created it. Now, for the first time, we ourselves can begin to draw a picture – of life in Predynastic Egypt. Excavations in the Nile Valley, some of them still ongoing, have started to answer many of our questions concerning daily life in Egypt's prehistoric past. Let us see what sort of a world those remote ancestors of the pharaohs inhabited.

First of all, Egypt in 4000 BC would have looked rather different from Egypt today. As we have already discovered, what is now desert bordering the Nile Valley on both sides would have been grassland in Predynastic times. Resembling the great plains of East Africa, the high plateau to the west of the Nile and the broad wadis to the east would have supported large, roaming herds of game animals. Elephants, giraffes, ostriches, and gazelles, probably even the occasional zebra and rhinoceros, would have been a familiar sight for people wandering through the savannah lands.

In the summer, after the rains, the dry grassland would have been transformed into lush grazing, attracting herders from the Nile Valley with their cattle. Just as in East Africa today, we can imagine vultures circling overhead, waiting for a kill, or gathering to roost on the thorny trees that dotted the landscape. There would have been other unwelcome companions in the height of summer. Snakes, emerged from their holes at the end of their hibernation, were an ever-present danger to people and young animals alike. Scorpions, too, lurked under rocks during the heat of the day, becoming active at night. The grassland was an abundant but dangerous environment, requiring vigilance by all its various inhabitants in their struggle for survival.

Nor was life in the Nile Valley without its own challenges. Here, the river ran slowly northwards, bringing life and fertility to its banks, and attracting both human and animal life. Hippos and crocodiles were a constant danger for the people living on the riverbanks. The times of greatest vulnerability were during fishing expeditions and river crossings, made in lightweight and relatively flimsy craft. Such activities were a necessary part of everyday life; yet an unexpected encounter with a single aggressive hippo, let alone a herd, could spell disaster. Little wonder, then, that these early Egyptians venerated the hippopotamus as a figure of great power, and sought to tame it through art and magic.

Also revered, but as symbols of distant majesty, were the kites that soared overhead, riding the thermals, then swooping lower over the river as the sun set. Looking down on the Nile Valley, this bird's-eye view would have revealed a rather different landscape from today's. For a start, the river described a different course, following a more westerly channel, especially in the northern part of the Nile Valley. The river's edge was thickly vegetated with reed-beds of papyrus and sedge, providing nesting grounds for wading birds. Wild cats prowled in search of vulnerable hatchlings, while rodents tried to steal eggs out of the nests. On dry land, the constant source of fresh water ensured lush vegetation, but much of it had not yet been turned over to agriculture. There would have been a few cultivated plots of land, dotted here and there, but overall the impact of humans on the environment was still relatively small.

If this was true in the narrow Nile Valley, it was even more the case in the broad expanse of the Delta. Where the river channel divided into several large watercourses on the last leg of its journey to the Mediterranean, the land became marshy and, in parts, impenetrable. Small channels criss-crossed the landscape, breaking it up into pockets of swampland, choked with thickets of papyrus. Here, herons and other wading birds gorged on the abundant fish; but for humans, eking out a living in this challenging environment was difficult. The early Delta inhabitants lived an impoverished lifestyle compared to their southern neighbours in the Nile Valley. This was reflected in the relative simplicity of their arts and crafts, and in the poverty of their burials.

For the cattle-herders of Upper Egypt, life was lived according to the rhythm of the seasons. In the winter, their herds found lush grazing by the river's edge. But, after the summer rains came the annual inundation, a miraculous surge of water that started beyond the southern horizon and gradually swelled over a period of days until it burst the Nile's banks. This flooded the low-lying land on either side of the river, rendering it temporarily unusable for agriculture or pasturage, until the waters receded again. By contrast, the summer rains transformed the grasslands to the east; they now beckoned with fresh, young growth, attracting both people and animals. Groups would have moved out along the broad wadis in search of the best pastures. They left behind the fields where, during the winter and spring, they had watched crops grow tall under the rays of the strong Egyptian sun. Agriculture was practised on a relatively small scale, and again it depended upon the cycle of the seasons. The inundation brought temporary disruption to the floodplain, but also great wealth as it deposited its annual layer of silt over the land, giving new fertility to the soil. Predynastic Egyptians recognized the potential of the inundation. If properly harnessed, by digging channels to distribute the floodwater over a large area, it would bring both water and nutrients to the fields each year. So, in the weeks before the inundation, those early farmers in the most favourable areas would have been busy readying the irrigation channels and checking the dykes that served as flood defences. Once the floodwaters arrived, there was little to do until they receded again. Then, it was time to sow in the newly watered and fertilized soil. During the winter and spring, the crops grew until they were ready to be harvested in the early summer. Then the annual cycle began again.

These first farmers grew a variety of crops, including cereals – probably barley and a primitive wheat called emmer. Once it had been harvested, threshed and milled, the grain was almost certainly made into bread and a coarse, porridge-like beer, the twin staples of the Egyptian diet throughout pharaonic times. The early Egyptians also cultivated a variety of vegetables: peas, vetch, an ancestor of the water-melon, and berries from the Christ's-thorn bush (*Zizyphus spina-christi*). Predynastic grave goods often include clay models of garlic bulbs, so garlic was probably a regular and valued part of the diet. The main source of protein would have been fish from the river. Nile perch (*Tilapia*) was a particularly prized variety, but catfish were also commonly eaten. These could be supplemented if necessary by freshwater molluscs, but shellfish do not seem to have been widely consumed. Geese had already been domesticated, and their bones are found in some abundance in Predynastic settlements, suggesting that they were reared for their meat. Pigs were also kept in significant numbers, for slaughter – and this persisted into later times, even when the pig was deemed an unclean animal according to Egyptian religion. Other livestock included large numbers of sheep and goats; and cattle, which were the main index of wealth. As such, they were too precious to slaughter, except on rare religious occasions. As we have seen, the Predynastic Egyptians probably exploited cattle for their milk and blood rather than their meat. Collections of bones excavated from settlements of this period also generally contain large numbers from more surprising animals: gazelles. Although partial domestication cannot be ruled out (the Predynastic equivalent of farmed venison), it is more likely that the Egyptians hunted the wild gazelles that lived on the desert savannahs bordering the Nile Valley. They must have lived in large herds within relatively easy reach of the villages on the flood-plain. As such, gazelles would have been an important additional source of meat. This evidence reinforces the picture of interdependence between valley and grassland ecosystems, manifest in so many other aspects of Predynastic Egyptian culture.

Despite a fairly nutritious and balanced diet, prehistoric Egyptians nevertheless suffered from a variety of afflictions. Besides such common conditions as toothache, cataracts, arthritis, and congenital deformities, parasitic diseases like schistosomiasis would have taken their toll on the weak and vulnerable. Infant mortality was high, as was death of mothers in childbirth, and the average life expectancy for those who survived childhood was probably no higher than the early forties. Little wonder, then, that people's most fervent religious practices often centred on fertility and procreation – for the next generation was the only guarantee of individual and family survival in an age before state provision.

Life was certainly hard for Egyptians living in 4000 BC, but the rigours of daily survival did not prevent them developing, and perfecting, arts and crafts. Foremost among these was pottery-making. As early as the beginning of the fifth millennium, the people living in and near the Nile Valley had discovered how to turn the abundant deposits of alluvial clay into fine wares for storage and eating. The potter's wheel had not yet been invented, so the Predynastic Egyptians formed their pots by hand. Even so, the most accomplished potters were able to produce vessels with egg-shell thin walls, thanks to a combination of technical skill and the fineness of the prepared clay. These fine vessels were often coated with a metallic slip, later burnished after firing to give a polished finish. Such prestigious objects were highly prized, and would have been reserved for special usage. Everyday pottery, produced as and when it was needed, on a household scale, was a much coarser affair. Instead of being carefully prepared to produce a fine fabric, the clay for everyday pots was mixed with large amounts of straw to help bind it together. Fired at a fairly low temperature, in the uncontrolled and uneven conditions of a household fire, the result was crude, but perfectly adequate for short-term storage, preparation and consumption of food.

A few specialist potters had taken the bold step of becoming full-time craftsmen. No longer part-time farmers or herders, they were now dependent on their skills to earn a living – by exchanging their products for food and other essentials. It is a telling indication of Predynastic Egyptian society that one of the first-ever full-time professional craftsmen set up his pottery kiln, not in one of the villages, but next to one of the biggest cemeteries of the period, near the burgeoning town of Nekhen. For it was the dead – or, rather, those who buried them – who were his main market. He specialized in producing fine pots, not for daily use, but for burying in the grave – for the eternal use of the deceased. Of course, not everyone could afford to procure specially made pots for their tomb, or the tomb of a relative. But Egypt in 4000 BC, and especially the town of Nekhen, was a place where a certain section of the population was growing increasingly rich and powerful. Upper-class Egyptians, like their successors the world over, felt an overwhelming need to demonstrate their status by means of objects – objects for display during their lifetime, and for display at their burial. So it was that, in Predynastic Egypt, a market for prestige objects – and for the craftsmen who made them – began to develop.

Pottery was not the only type of craft production practised by an increasingly specialized workforce. Flint-working and stone-carving, too, were fast developing into activities of great skill. Since the dawn of time and the first arrival of humans in the Nile Valley, people had exploited flint to make tools and weapons: tips for harpoons, arrowheads, small blades for wood-working, and knives. At sites near the river in Middle Egypt, supplies of flint were both abundant and easily accessible. Once extracted from the rock – a fairly simple operation – the flint nodules swiftly found their way throughout the whole of the Nile Valley as they were traded from village to village.

Other types of stone were a different matter, however. Egypt is blessed with a dazzling variety of hard stones amenable to carving: smooth white and yellow limestones; reddish quartzite; pink and grey granites; dense greenish-grey siltstone; translucent, banded, honey-coloured calcite; black and white speckled diorite, to name but a few. In later times, the Egyptians were to become experts at stone-working, creating vessels, statues and buildings with a perfection that has never been surpassed. But in 4000 BC, craftsmanship in stone was still in its infancy. A major difficulty was mining the stone in the first place. Supplies of some rock types were not difficult to identify: for example, limestone is the dominant rock forming the cliffs either side of the Nile Valley, from the apex of the Delta as far south as the vicinity of Nekhen; granite boulders form the natural barrier in the course of the Nile known as the First Cataract, the traditional border between Egypt and Nubia. But other, more exotic rocks were far less accessible, occurring only in isolated outcrops in remote regions far from the Nile Valley. The logistics of organizing expeditions to obtain supplies of these stones were far from straightforward, and would have posed real challenges to a society still largely structured at the village level. Only local rulers with the necessary manpower and resources could realistically have sponsored mining expeditions to these distant quarries. And so, it is primarily in high-status contexts that most of the early stone objects are found.

Even if a mining expedition could be organized, the task of prising workable blocks of stone free from the bedrock was a daunting task in a society without metal tools. A hand-held pounder – a ball of stone harder than the one being quarried – would have been a quarryman's main tool. It is scarcely surprising that large-scale sculpture is unknown in early Predynastic times; it only became feasible with the widespread adoption of metal tools some centuries later. For the most part, small blocks of stone – many of them probably naturally occurring boulders – seem to have been used. In any case, stone objects were clearly highly prized and valuable objects, usually reserved for the wealthier and more powerful members of Egyptian society.

A notable exception was the category of object known as palettes. At its simplest, a palette was a flat, smooth piece of stone on which mineral pigment could be ground to produce face-paint. As we have seen, the use of palettes dates back to the earliest Predynastic times, so that by 4000 BC they had evolved over perhaps a thousand years. As well as the simple, lozenge-shaped palettes so characteristic of this period, craftsmen had also begun to produce ever-more elaborate animal-shaped forms, reflecting both the Egyptians' fascination with the natural world and their familiarity with the fauna of the savannah. Palettes in the shape of wild goats, antelope, turtles, hippos, and even elephants are all known from Predynastic sites. The favoured stone for making palettes was the fine-grained, greenish-grey stone known variously as siltstone, schist, or sometimes (incorrectly) slate. For centuries, supplies of siltstone had been obtained from the Black Mountains, in the heart of the Red Sea hills. Individual cattle-herders or perhaps small bands of men must have made regular trips to this dramatic area, to prise away conveniently sized pieces of rock which they could then carry back to their villages to be turned into palettes. Many a hut or fireside in Predynastic Egypt must have echoed to the chip-chip-chip of flint and stone tools, as craftsmen patiently fashioned the palettes which, 6,000 years later, adorn the display cases of museums worldwide.

When not carving stone, the same simple tools could be used by craftsmen to work other materials, especially wood and ivory. Because of its fragility, wood has not survived very well from distant antiquity; but it would have been the most common material for the Predynastic craftsmen, and we may imagine that it was widely used – for combs and other ornaments, for a variety of small implements, and even for children's toys. Ivory, from hippos and elephants, was altogether rarer and more valuable. It was used for finely detailed figurines and small vases. Like stone vessels, these ivory objects were highly prized and beyond the means of all but the wealthiest members of society.

In 4000 BC, most Egyptians lived in small communities, probably organized along tribal lines. Each community comprised a group of extended families, and numbered between 50 and 200 individuals in total. During the summer months, people followed their herds away from the Nile Valley, heading for the grasslands of the eastern savannah. Towards the end of the summer, as the new season's fodder grew scarcer, the journey was made in the opposite direction, back to the security and permanent pasture of the Nile Valley. During the winter months, home for the average Predynastic Egyptian was a small, semi-permanent village, situated at the edge of the floodplain, enjoying a slightly elevated view of the river and beyond the reach of the inundation. Villages were also sited to take advantage of both ecological zones: the alluvial land and the drier savannah. Settlements consisted of a cluster of small, round huts, made from wooden posts and matting to keep out the wind. Most families had their own hearth, situated just outside the hut, on which food was prepared, and which provided the only source of warmth on a chill winter's night. Huts were too small to have separate rooms. Instead, all family members slept together, in the single round space. Other activities were carried out in the open air, including pottery-making and other crafts, food production, and the social interaction that characterizes village life. Life was, no doubt, as full of individual triumphs and tragedies, of laughter and tears, of intrigue and gossip, as it is in any small community today.

Each village had its headman, who took decisions on behalf of the community and perhaps controlled some of its communal wealth. In earlier times, headmen had been chosen by the members of the community; but by 4000 BC, there are signs that authority was becoming hereditary, passed from generation to generation by powerful local families. The evidence for inherited status comes in the form of wealthy child burials, which appear around 4000 BC for the first time. The fact that a community would invest more time, energy and resources in the burial of an infant than in the burials of many adults clearly indicates that prestige could be ascribed at birth rather than achieved through actions. Of course, hereditary authority was one of the hallmarks of classic Egyptian civilization, with the king at its apex. We now know that communities living a thousand years before the unification of the country were taking the first steps towards the creation of a complex society with clearly defined social classes.

However, birth was not the only way of achieving status in a Predynastic village. Great reverence was also reserved for the shamans: men – and quite possibly women as well – who possessed the ability to make contact with the spirit world. At births and deaths, at important festivals and moments of crisis for the village, these spiritual figures could enter trance-like states, to commune with the supernatural forces that controlled the lives of ordinary people. As a result, they were powerful and respected individuals. Many of them were buried with trappings of authority, such as ivory tags, and the clay figurines they may have used during rituals, to accompany them into the world beyond the grave.

Burial of the dead was a vital act, not only for the deceased person, but also for those left behind. Proper preparation for the afterlife journey was essential, both for the eternal survival of the departed, and for the prosperity of the whole community. For the dead took with them into the spirit world the hopes and fears of their families and neighbours. If the village were to survive and flourish, the newly departed needed to be given a proper send-off: grave goods to accompany them into the hereafter; spells and prayers to be recited over the burial to ward off evil forces; rituals and festivities to allow the survivors to come to terms with their loss and regain their sense of cohesion.

If death was an ever-present threat, Predynastic Egyptians did not have to deal with some of the other pressures faced by their descendants 6,000 years later. For example, space was not a problem, and each community carefully set aside a special area, beyond the village, for burial. Demarcation of the living and the dead was important for both groups. The local cemetery was near enough to allow regular visits by relatives to the grave-side; far enough away from the huts to allow people to carry on their lives without constant reminders of bereavement. Nevertheless, life and death were closely knit in Predynastic Egypt, the spirit world never far away in the constant struggle for survival.

While semi-nomadic village life was all that most people knew, there was already a small handful of larger settlements, strung out along the river. Here, the rhythm of life and the structure of society were different, and becoming more so with each passing generation. At Nekhen in the southernmost part of the Egyptian Nile Valley, as at the place called Nubt further to the north, a combination of strategic economic factors had favoured the establishment of a town. In both localities, there were still scatters of small villages, but increasingly, the town acted as a magnet for the surrounding population. It offered greater security, and greater opportunities for employment, especially for the growing numbers of specialist craftsmen who depended on their skills to support themselves and their families. Another emerging centre of population – and power – was the town of Tjeni, in the northern part of Upper Egypt. It was located on the west bank of the Nile and lay directly opposite the point where the eastern cliffs come closest to the river, forming a natural constriction. This strategic location gave the rulers of Tjeni effective control over river traffic passing through their region. Added to this important economic advantage was the proximity of routes leading across the western savannah. The main tracks from the Nile Valley to the western oases left the cultivation in the vicinity of Tjeni. Rare commodities from the western region, especially stones, thus naturally fell under the control of Tjeni's rulers. These same individuals also enjoyed direct access to the southern Nile Valley, thanks to the routes which cut across the western savannah, bypassing the great Qena bend in the Nile. This would have significantly reduced the time taken to reach southern Egypt with its own important resources. These routes were to prove crucial to the rulers of Tjeni in the unification of Egypt a thousand years later.

Whereas Tjeni drew its strength from connections with the west, the foundation and subsequent prosperity of both Nekhen and Nubt depended on the resources of the eastern savannah – on gold, to be precise. Nubt, whose very name in Egyptian meant 'the golden', was located opposite the entrance to the Wadi Hammamat. This broad valley, one of the two principal east–west routes from the Nile Valley to the Red Sea, led directly to the gold mines of Bir Umm Fawakhir, just beyond the Black Mountains. In early Predynastic times, it is likely that the local village rulers of Nubt gained political and economic advantage from their control of gold-mining activity in the Wadi Hammamat. Over the years, they and their community came to dominate the surrounding region. Wealth brought with it patronage, increased economic activity, enhanced employment opportunities, and a growing population. It also brought a desire for control – of resources and

people. And so was born the ancient Egyptian obsession with bureaucracy, as the early chiefs of Nubt sought to turn economic advantage
into political power.

Further south, the rise of Nekhen was also connected with control
of the gold trade. Opposite the town, the Wadi Abbad led to gold mines
of the Wadi Barramiya. Exploiting this strategic advantage, the early
chiefs of Nekhen grew wealthy and influential. This gave them the
power of patronage, reflected in the fact that the earliest known specialist potter set up shop at Nekhen. As the town grew in size and
importance, the hereditary village headmen began to accrue to themselves greater prestige; at the same time, they began to set themselves
apart, psychologically and physically, from their fellow inhabitants.
Nowhere is this better illustrated than in the tombs of these Predynastic rulers. They were built in a special, exclusive cemetery, remote from
the town and the burial-ground of the local population. In their size
and contents, they outstripped even the largest private tomb.

Throughout history, powerful men and women have sought to distinguish themselves in death, as well as in life, from their subjects.
Today's state funerals must have had their counterparts for the rulers of
the ancient world, but the rituals that accompanied the death of a powerful individual have left little or no trace in the archaeological record.
Instead, we rely on the material remains: the tombs themselves. In
Egypt today, the cliff-top mausoleum of the Aga Khan at Aswan, and
the marble-clad tomb of the Shah of Iran in a Cairo mosque are but
two examples. So also, in Egypt 6,000 years ago, rulers were interred in
sumptuous burials, furnished with prestigious objects: decorated
pottery bowls imported from Nubia; ostrich eggs; stone vases; and jewellery. A local chieftain at Gebelein, near modern Luxor, was buried
with a unique painted cloth, decorated with ritual and religious scenes,
probably intended to assist the deceased in the afterlife. At Abadiya, situated at the northern end of the great Qena bend in the Nile, the ruler
was interred in great splendour in one of the richest tombs of the
period. As we have seen in Chapter 3, his tomb contained a truly dazzling array of objects: six clay figurines of women, and three clay

models of hippos; two pink limestone pendants in the shape of hippos; no fewer than fifteen pottery vessels, including one in the shape of a woman, one modelled as a fish, one incised with the figure of an antelope, and two rare vases based on the design of contemporary stone vessels; four cosmetic palettes, one of them in the form of a large hippo with an inlaid shell eye; nine bracelets of hippo ivory and one of elephant ivory; three combs and four complete tusks of hippo ivory; four bracelets, three combs and a hairpin made from bone; 411 clay beads for jewellery, 144 beads of carnelian, and one bead of glazed steatite; six model ostrich eggs made of whitened clay; six clay tokens, possibly used for accounting purposes (and reflecting the tomb owner's economic as well as political power); a chunk of fragrant resin; and two fragments of green malachite from the mountains of Sinai. To call such tombs 'royal' is no exaggeration. Symbols of office buried with the deceased hint at their political power: stone maceheads may have been carried as purely ceremonial objects, like royal sceptres in monarchies today, but they would have been equally effective as weapons of aggression, beating any opposition into submission. Egyptian society was already dividing into the rulers and those they ruled.

One of the hallmarks of power is the ability to command scarce resources and, in particular, the acquisition of exotic objects. The Predynastic rulers of Nekhen were no exception. Some were even buried with exotic animals – lions and elephants. Perhaps they had been kept as pets in the ruler's private zoo. Certainly, they were a reminder of the eastern savannah, the ultimate source of Nekhen's wealth and prestige. If trade had made the rulers of Nekhen what they were, it was magnificently reflected in their grave goods, which included lapis lazuli brought from the far away Afghan mountains. Humbler, though no less exotic to the eyes of Upper Egyptians, were the pottery vessels – their contents unknown but doubtless highly valued – imported from distant northern Egypt. For the inhabitants of Nekhen and Nubt, the lower reaches of the Nile and the marshy swamplands of the Delta were unknown territory. Where the great river divided into the channels that flowed towards the Mediterranean Sea, the familiar environment of floodplain and savannah gave way to a strange and confusing landscape. Low-lying fields were criss-crossed by myriad waterways, making transport and communication difficult. The local people spoke with a distinctive accent, and their customs were equally curious. Instead of burying their dead with abundant supplies for the afterlife, a few simple pots were thought sufficient. Perhaps the prayers that were spoken over the grave played a more important role – in any case, the typical Upper Egyptian was probably as ignorant of life in Predynastic Lower Egypt as we are today.

One outstanding feature of Lower Egyptian society in 4000 BC is known, however. Despite their relative poverty, the people of the lower Nile and Delta were active traders. They not only made the most of their strategic proximity to Palestine – the source of many of the luxury commodities destined for the rulers of Upper Egypt – but they also welcomed communities of foreign traders into their midst. A striking example was the small village of Maadi, situated on the east bank of the Nile, just south of the apex of the Delta. Here the inhabitants lived in simple wooden and reed huts, just like their southern neighbours. They, too, exploited the twin ecological zones in the vicinity: the lush vegetation of the floodplain and the grazing land of the savannah. More important than farming or cattle-herding, however, was trade. Behind the village, the Wadi Digla led eastwards towards the Great Bitter Lakes, the Gulf of Suez, thence to the Sinai peninsula and Palestine beyond. Maadi lay at the Nile Valley end of this trade route, and the villagers exchanged locally produced commodities for a range of foreign imports. Most notable among them was a radical new material from the hills of southern Palestine: copper. The people of Maadi developed an early mastery of copper-working, smelting the raw ore into ingots. Thus, in a small northern village, began the era of metal-working in Egypt, centuries before it caught on in the prosperous towns of Upper Egypt.

Maadi lived by trade, and this brought the locals into direct contact with their trading partners. In an area on the northwestern edge of the village, a resident group of Palestinians had set up their homes. This immigrant community steadfastly maintained its own culture and way of life. The houses were constructed in the contemporary Palestinian style, partially sunk into the ground and covered with a framework of wood and matting. The immigrants even made their flint tools according to the traditional Palestinian method. Yet they seem to have enjoyed good relations with their Egyptian hosts, so both communities must have benefited from the arrangement.

Another flourishing Palestinian community lived in the town of Dep, in the far northwest of the Delta, on the Mediterranean coast. Here, the immigrant potters manufactured their fine, V-shaped bowls, just like their compatriots back in southern Palestine. They used a slow turning device – a sort of primitive potter's wheel – to achieve the bowls' outward-flaring shape and thin walls. This technology was far superior to that being used by the local Egyptian potters, who still formed their vessels entirely by hand before firing them – rather unevenly, in a badly-regulated furnace. Remarkably, the Egyptians did not copy the visitors' more advanced techniques, but soldiered on in their own way. The slow potter's wheel was not adopted in Egypt for another thousand years. Whether this illustrates the relative isolation of the Palestinian community at Dep, or the innate conservatism of the Egyptians – or both – is hard to say. It certainly confirms that Lower Egypt in the Predynastic period was a remarkably cosmopolitan place, in which Egyptians and Palestinians regularly rubbed shoulders. In this respect, the north was a very different place from the upper Nile Valley, where people's horizons extended eastwards towards the Red Sea hills rather than northwards towards foreign lands.

~ · ~ · ~

To return, then, to the question at the beginning of this chapter: what was life like in Egypt in 4000 BC? It very much depended on where you lived. If you were born and grew up in the Nile Delta, your view of the world – and Egypt's place in it – may well have been very different from that of your Upper Egyptian contemporary. Since our story – of the Eastern Desert rock art and its creators – concerns the inhabitants of the southern Nile Valley and the savannah lands to the east, we will finish this survey of life before the pharaohs by following the life of one fictional man and his family, from the Nekhen region of Upper Egypt. The invention of writing was still nearly a thousand years in the future, so we can only guess at the names given to Egyptians in 4000 BC. For the sake of argument, let us call our character Sen – ancient Egyptian for 'brother'.

~ · ~ · ~

Sen was born, 6,000 years ago, in a small village on the east bank of the Nile, in the deep south of Egypt. Great anticipation had surrounded his birth: he was his parents' second child, and his mother had nearly died after her first baby was born. Sen's aunt – whom he was never to know – had died in childbirth just a year before. Such things were common, and Sen's whole family was deeply anxious for mother and baby this time around. For some time before the birth, prayers had been offered to the gods, and spells recited to ward off evil forces. When it came to the moment of delivery, the village shaman, a distant cousin of Sen's, conducted rituals with a small fertility figurine carved from hippopotamus ivory. The womenfolk gathered around Sen's mother, dancing, shouting and playing bone castanets to drive away any malevolent spirits. The male relatives, banned from attending the birth, sat at some distance around a hearth, and talked in hushed tones as they awaited news of the birth. It was winter, and Sen's family, like the others in the community, were living in their village overlooking the Nile Valley. The crude wooden and wickerwork huts afforded some protection from the cooler nights, but a fire was still welcome.

One of the elder female relatives broke the news: the birth had been successful; the baby was a boy. The news spread fast around the community. Family and friends were relieved and joyful. Sen's first few months were spent in the relative seclusion of the village. His father and uncles spent the day tending their animals in the lush fields by the

Nile. His mother, assisted by her sisters, suckled her two children while carrying out the daily tasks. She made simple hand-made pots from supplies of clay brought from the river bank. These were fired over the family hearth which also served to cook the food. The family's diet was simple: milk from the cattle and fish caught daily in the Nile, supplemented by vegetables and a coarse bread. It was meagre, but sufficient. If he survived his first few years – and many babies did not – Sen could look forward to a life of perhaps thirty or forty years.

Before he was even six months old, however, Sen's world was thrown upside down. The summer rains had just arrived, and with them the inundation. The land by the river's edge was flooded, and it was time for the village to follow its livestock to the fresh new grazing on the eastern savannah. As the embers of the last fire died away, the villagers and their animals headed off eastwards, walking at the pace of the slowest. They would spend the next few months on the move, and they took only the bare essentials with them: a few pottery vessels (clay was scarce in the savannah lands), amulets and small items of personal adornment, and of course the siltstone palettes that played so central a part in the rituals of the community.

The villagers struck out along the Wadi Abbad. They had come this way as long as anyone could remember. It was, for them as for their descendants centuries hence, the gateway to another world: the eastern savannah. Certainly, the terrain here was very different from the Nile Valley. The wide wadi floor was strewn with rocks; these presented no difficulty to the livestock, but people had to pick their way more carefully to avoid a fall or a sprain. As the group passed a huge, towering rock on the northern side of the wadi, Sen's mother noticed the carvings which adorned one of its smooth faces. These she knew to be of great significance – echoes of magical rituals that concerned the community's survival, now and in the next world.

A day later, with the Nile Valley already out of sight, the group entered the familiar, narrow wadi that stretched to the eastern horizon. One or two of the older and more experienced members of the community knew that it led all the way to the gold mines, past ranges of mountains, to the sea. But that was not the destination this time. After a few days' travelling eastwards, the small band of people and animals branched off to the north, along a much wider wadi. Here there was good grazing for the animals, but better still lay ahead. Two full weeks after leaving their village, Sen and his extended family entered the mouth of the wadi that he was to visit, each year, for the rest of his life. Its narrow floor afforded good grazing (see Plate 7), but equally important, protection for the community's precious herds. Natural rock shelters offered welcome rest from the heat of the summer sun. There was abundant game here and in other neighbouring wadis – ostrich, antelope and ibex, giraffes, even elephants. Hunting would be an important part of life for the menfolk over the next few months.

The group made camp at the mouth of the wadi, under a rock overhang. This at least gave them some protection from wild animals and, just as important, offered shade during the intense heat of the day. From dawn to dusk, while the men hunted or tended the livestock, Sen and his mother spent the long hours in camp, taking refuge from the sun, occasionally venturing out to gather foodplants and firewood. At dusk, the men would return and the extended family would gather around the hearth listening to stories about the day's exploits – just as they did in their village by the banks of the Nile.

After a few months in the savannah, the grazing began to get more scarce. Sen's family had to break camp with increasing frequency as they followed the animals in search of new pasturage. Eventually, the decision was taken: it was time to return to the Nile Valley where the well-watered fields would provide more reliable food for the livestock. Sen's first summer had come to an end.

As he grew from baby into boy, Sen was to live out this constant, unchanging rhythm: winter and spring in the Nile Valley, summer and early autumn in the eastern savannah. Both environments held excitements and challenges. Sen would have to learn to cope with two radically different worlds if he were to survive and prosper into adulthood. He would need to learn about the dangerous wild animals that posed a constant threat to the unwary. Fierce hippos lived in the Nile and could easily upturn a small fishing boat, killing its occupants. True, the village shaman regularly said spells to guard against such a disaster – and people sought to master the beast's power by painting its likeness on their finest pottery. None the less, Sen was careful whenever he went fishing with his father, or crossed the river in a small reed boat, for there were crocodiles to watch out for as well. Out on the grasslands in summer, snakes and scorpions were the greatest danger. Once again, the magic power of art was harnessed to keep such threats at bay – Sen recalled the images the elders made on rocks out in the savannah.

Like the other information he would need to survive life, Sen acquired most of his knowledge about the natural world from his parents and friends, and from his own personal experiences. There was no formal schooling, but advice was regularly given by the adults – and swiftly taken on board by the younger members of the village. Egypt in 4000 BC was a difficult and dangerous place; learning from one's experiences often made the difference between life and death. Accidents did happen, of course, and there were powerful herbal remedies for some injuries and diseases. But all too often, a bad fall or a snake bite resulted in death. During his early years, Sen saw friends and relatives plucked from their community in the prime of life. He did not rail against this – it was simply part and parcel of the natural order. For people as well as animals, life and death were never far apart.

Fortunately, Sen survived the perils of childhood and, in time, started his own family (Fig. 42). In the space of less than twenty years, he found himself changed from newborn infant to father, from the newest member of his community to one of its respected elders. Others now turned to him as a source of advice and practical experience. He now led his family on its annual journey from Nile to savannah and back again. During the summer months, far from resting with his mother in the shade of a rock overhang, Sen now accompanied the livestock on its foragings and joined the other men on hunting expeditions. He also took part in the spiritual life of his community, in particular creating the ritual images that expressed the complex interrelationship of human, natural and supernatural worlds.

As he and his companions prepared for the hunt, or while lying in wait for the herds of game to pass by, Sen would create images of the hunters and the animals they hunted. He hoped that his wishes for a successful outcome, once made real in art, would translate into reality by magical assistance. But not all of Sen's rock art concerned the hunt. He also sought through the power of art to express the inexpressible: the nature of the spirit world and the mysteries of life after death. Like the animal and human spheres that met in the drama of the hunt, the natural and supernatural spheres were constant companions. Their complex interactions shaped Sen's very existence and the world around him. In turn, Sen and his companions gave expression to their hopes, fears and deepest beliefs through words and songs – which have long since vanished – and in pictures.

In a secret place near the mouth of the wadi where he had passed his very first summer, on a large, vertical rock face hidden from view, Sen added his own images to a canvas that had been built up over generations. Huge giraffes towered over the scene, their tall bodies and outstretched necks seeming to link the earth and the heavens. All around were images of the wild animals of Sen's world: the ostrich and ibex of the eastern savannah, the hippos of the Nile Valley. Over the

42 *A hunter and his family, Wadi Mineh. Family groups like this are comparatively rare in the Eastern Desert rock art, but they convey a strong sense of the social ties that bound prehistoric Egyptian society together.*

course of several days, with nothing but a small sharp stone, Sen pecked into the rock face his own contribution to this great religious tableau. He carefully drew a boat with many oars. But this was no ordinary boat; it was a superhuman version of the craft he regularly encountered on the river. Sen had occasionally seen similar designs on painted pottery, but pots did not last. By contrast, etched into the living rock, Sen's boat was for eternity. Indeed, its symbolism went to the very heart of Sen's beliefs. Since he had first listened to the village elders and observed the rituals performed by the local shaman at moments of importance or crisis – births, deaths, the changes of season – he had begun to sense the mystery of what lay beyond the grave. Life was a journey, and Sen did not doubt the journey would continue after his death – a miraculous journey, through a spirit world inhabited by gods and monsters.

Even as he watched his own children grow into adults, Sen remained keenly aware of the transitoriness of his earthly existence. He had no doubt that the objects he had seen placed in the tombs of the departed – jars of food and drink, charms and amulets to ward off evil spirits, a few treasured earthly possessions – would certainly be needed in the hereafter. He hoped and trusted that he too, when death came, would be laid to rest with the necessary rites, and buried with the provisions to help him on his way, wherever that way might lead.

5

SHIPS OF THE DESERT
The Birth of the Egyptian Religion

W hy did the people of prehistoric Egypt go to the trouble of carving images on rocks? What ultimate purpose did the petroglyphs serve? The answers to these fundamental questions will take us to the heart of the ancient Egyptian psyche, and will bring us face-to-face with the most intriguing images yet discovered in the Eastern Desert.

To the modern, especially the Western mind, art is something that is created above all for aesthetic reasons. Paintings, sculptures, ceramics and textiles: all are fashioned by artists to express their own creativity and to stir the feelings of the viewer. Indeed, the very word 'art' carries connotations of skill and imagination, but also of decorative intent. By contrast, the ancient Egyptians had no word for 'art'. The concept of 'art for art's sake' was, it seems, wholly unknown to them. Instead, the underlying purpose of ancient Egyptian art – especially the art commissioned by the king and his courtiers for their homes and tombs – was what we might call magical or religious. For example, by reducing a wild animal to a series of artist's strokes, the Egyptians believed they could achieve power over it: mastery through depiction. On another level, to show something in picture form was to make it permanent and ensure its survival for all eternity. (This was also the thinking behind hieroglyphic writing, itself a series of pictures.) So the familiar scenes inscribed on the walls of Egyptian temples, showing the king making offerings to the gods, were designed, not to record what went on in the temple, but rather to ensure that these rituals would continue, and would be properly carried out, for ever.

Once this underlying philosophy is properly appreciated, it casts new light on some familiar examples of ancient Egyptian art. In private tombs from all periods of Egyptian history, some of the most fascinating scenes are those commonly called 'scenes of daily life'. These include scenes of baking and brewing, of craftsmen making pottery and furniture, of harvesting and winnowing, and scenes of the tomb owner carrying out his duties ('his', because the owners of decorated tombs in ancient Egypt were nearly always men). Ever since archaeologists first discovered such paintings, people have remarked on their amazing attention to detail. Indeed, it is only thanks to scenes of craftsmen at work that we know as much as we do about ancient Egyptian technology. While these scenes are surely one of our best sources of evidence for life in ancient Egypt, it is nevertheless a mistake to label them 'scenes of daily life'. For they were not included in the tomb decoration primarily as a record of earthly existence. Rather, their purpose was to ensure that the tomb owner's idealized view of the world – his own personal Utopia – would continue for eternity, for the benefit of his reborn and undying spirit. The carefully executed scenes of baking and brewing had but one purpose: to guarantee a perpetual supply of bread and beer (the staples of the ancient Egyptian diet) for the afterlife. Even if the real food and drink buried in the tomb should be destroyed or used up, the scenes on the tomb walls would magically ensure a never-ending supply. Agricultural scenes were a further insurance policy, ensuring an eternal source of the basic ingredient for baking and brewing, barley. The scenes of craftsmen at work served a similar purpose. They guaranteed that the tomb-owner would enjoy his afterlife with all the necessary creature comforts, even if the grave goods should perish.

Even tomb paintings showing the owner carrying out his

responsibilities – whether counting cattle or giving legal judgments – were created, not to record the details of daily life, but with a view to the afterlife. Look more closely at such scenes, and you will find their view of life is far from realistic. Absent are the disease and dirt that must have been an ever-present feature of ancient Egyptian life, in the towns as in the countryside. Absent, too, are the crucial episodes in anybody's life: births, marriages and deaths. Instead, the scenes are presented in a timeless and highly idealized fashion. The tomb-owner is always shown at his most vigorous and authoritative. Members of his family – his wife and children – are shown in subordinate roles, fulfilling their ideal duties with respect to the owner, but without independent existence as real people. So-called scenes of daily life do not show life as it really was – but life as the tomb-owners (who were generally members of the ruling class) would have liked it to be; and, more importantly, life as they wanted it to be in the hereafter.

Consider, also, the famous scenes of 'leisure pursuits' included in many private tombs, especially hunting by boat in the papyrus marshes and (in tombs of the New Kingdom) hunting by chariot in the desert. Do these really record what the tomb-owners did on their days off, or do they serve a different purpose? If we bear in mind their location – the tomb, place of rebirth and eternal existence – and if we look in detail at their symbolism, their underlying significance becomes clear. The scenes of hunting in the marshes, in particular, are laden with religious symbols. Hippopotamus hunting symbolized the defeat of chaos, essential if the tomb-owner's spirit were to be successfully reborn in the afterlife. Fish are also frequently shown being speared. In ancient Egyptian, the word 'to spear (a fish)' is the same as the word 'to impregnate'. The sexual symbolism of fishing was designed to create the right atmosphere for the dead person's rebirth in the tomb. The same is true

43 *Human figure, perhaps a shaman, Wadi Abu Wasil. The wild hair may indicate that the person is in a state of trance. Petroglyphs like this provide rare insights into the religious practices of the early Egyptians.*

of the ducks that are often shown being held by the tomb-owner or his wife. Ducks were – and still are – associated with sexual energy. What may appear to us at first sight as a pleasant scene from a weekend outing would, to the ancient Egyptian who commissioned it, have been a powerful network of symbols, all cooperating to help in his eventual rebirth. In the same way, scenes of hunting in the desert served as a strong metaphor for the battle between order and chaos, good and evil. Order and good always triumph – at least in the paintings.

These examples all serve to make the crucial point: Egyptian art was, in essence, religious. This is true throughout Egyptian history, and indeed prehistory. With this understanding, we can begin to unlock the true significance of the Eastern Desert petroglyphs.

First, let us broaden our view for a moment. Rock art is a worldwide phenomenon. Long before the Eastern Desert images came to light, similar echoes from prehistory were well known at locations throughout the world. From the caves of Lascaux in France and Altamira in northern Spain to the rock-shelters of the Arnhem Land in Australia's Northern Territory, rock art provides a tantalizing glimpse into the minds of our remote ancestors. Just as all humans alive today share the same basic feelings and emotions – encapsulated in the well-known phrase 'what unites us is greater than what divides us' – so the rock art produced by people of distant times and places shares much in common. For example, hunting is a common theme. At many rock art sites, scenes seem to reflect the trance-like dreams of shamans. As far as the petroglyphs of Egypt's Eastern Desert are concerned, this shamanistic interpretation is particularly attractive when considering Site 26 in the Wadi Abu Wasil. At one place, a prominent flat rock that is literally covered in images, the human figures are shown with strange braided hair, sticking up on end like the teeth of a comb (Fig. 43). It is tempting to think that they represent shamans during the trance, or altered state of consciousness, that allowed practitioners to make temporary contact with the sacred realm. In such cases the rock art would have marked a desire to bridge the natural and supernatural worlds, to preserve a permanent reminder of another dimension. Rocks were particularly good places to create such images, because they could themselves be gateways to the spirit world. A cliff face or cave wall was not simply a blank canvas, waiting to be decorated. It was, in the eyes of many cultures, a place where the humans that walked the earth and the spirits that dwelled within it could communicate – or at least commune.

It is no coincidence that some of the greatest concentrations of rock art in the Eastern Desert occur in shaded and partially hidden places: cliff overhangs, rock-shelters, and the like (Plate 3). Not only do these places afford some protection from the heat of the sun, which must have been intense during the middle of the day, even in prehistoric times; they also, and perhaps more importantly, offer seclusion. They are places where people could withdraw, at least partially, from the natural world, to commune with the supernatural. In other words, they are places where a spiritually charged atmosphere was more easily invoked. While we shall never know exactly who made the petroglyphs in the Eastern Desert, nor in what circumstances, it seems very likely that they were made during the course of magical or religious ceremonies. They may even have been created by shamans in a state of trance, or at least by elders of the community with some degree of spiritual authority.

The images themselves fall into two major categories: scenes suggesting domination of the animal world (whether by tethering cattle or by hunting wild beasts); and boats. In many ways, the theme of animal domination is the more familiar one from later Egyptian religion, and will serve as a useful entry point into the minds and motivations of the ancient artists. As we have already seen, cattle played a central role in the culture of Egyptians living in 4000 BC. The imagery of the bull was already firmly established at this time – in pottery, amulets and animal-shaped cosmetic palettes. It was to remain central to Egyptian art for millennia. While the wild bull symbolized the forces of nature at their most aggressive – which could be embodied in the person of the divine king – the tamed bull was an equally powerful metaphor. It stood for the triumph of the human will over these same unruly and potentially destructive forces. So, in Egyptian art from prehistoric times, the simple motif of cattle husbandry became symbolically charged. As we shall see in Chapter 6, many of the items of royal regalia familiar from ancient Egypt, such as the crook, the flail and the strangely shaped animal-headed was-sceptre, originated as implements used by cattle-herders and shepherds to control their livestock. Their symbolic associations were powerful enough for them to make the seamless transition from pasture to palace.

So, the images of tethered cattle in the Eastern Desert rock art are not, perhaps, merely representations of a way of life. They are also expressions of will: the imposition of order and control on the potentially unruly forces of nature. They express an idealized view of the cosmos, where supernatural forces assisted humans in overcoming natural forces. Nowhere is this better illustrated than in one of the motifs on the main wall near the 'jacuzzi' in the Wadi Umm Salam. Here, the figure holding a tethered bull is distinguished by a head-dress of two tall plumes. As we shall see later, this was the quintessential mark of divinity. It identifies the cattle-controller as a god, magically assisting the human herders who created the drawing in their domination of the animal world.

The same fundamental attitude underlies the frequent scenes of hunting. Here, the relationship between the human agents and their animal opponents is more dynamic. In a striking, and rare, example of the hippopotamus hunting motif, pecked into the side wall of an inaccessible rock overhang in the Wadi Mineh, the hippo is shown already laid low by the harpoon, while the hunter, standing at some distance, has launched a further weapon – this time a spear – to finish the job. The spear is depicted in mid-flight, sailing through the air between the hunter and his quarry. The animal is being assaulted on two fronts, to ensure the victory of the human protagonist. In this way, order is imposed through the active defeat of chaos, symbolized by the hunting expedition. We find this theme in later periods of Egyptian art, such as the famous painted box from the tomb of Tutankhamun. On this object, there is a deliberate and striking contrast between the orderly depiction of the king in his chariot and the confused mass of wild animals (or foreign enemies) arrayed before him. In prehistoric art, the hippo is felled by the hunter's harpoon; ibex and gazelle are brought down by hunting-dogs or by their masters' arrows. The idealized outcome is never in doubt. Humans will triumph because the gods are with them. Indeed, this was probably the principal purpose of the drawings themselves: to encourage divine assistance in the hunt and thereby to ensure a successful outcome. By giving the desired outcome permanence, in the form of a picture, half the battle had already been won. Art and magic were closely interlinked: just as tomb paintings of bakers and brewers could 'come to life' in the afterlife, so images of a successful hunt could magically bring success when it came to the real thing. The hunter had already mastered his quarry by reducing it to a series of artist's strokes. Its certain defeat was all but guaranteed.

There was also another, equally powerful weapon in the hunters' armoury: sympathetic magic. The Egyptians, like many other peoples the world over, believed that people could assume the qualities of an animal by wearing part of it in their costume. So, for example, in dynastic times, the king was shown wearing a bull's tail, tucked into the back of his waist-band. The symbolism was clear: the bull's tail gave the king the power of the bull. It brought him the beast's strength, virility and aggressive potential. In the same way, the hunters shown on a cere-monial palette from the end of the Predynastic period wear the tails of hunting-dogs. They thereby gained the animals' swiftness and determi-nation (literally 'doggedness'), an essential quality if their hunt was to

44 *Hunters wearing horns, Wadi Abu Wasil. A common practice among shamanistic peoples worldwide is the wearing of animal attributes, especially horns, during religious rituals. According to Egyptian beliefs, horns would magically endow the wearer with the qualities of an antelope (swiftness and agility), and would help the hunter to triumph over his quarry.*

be successful. In the rock art, the hunters of the eastern savannah are often shown wearing attributes, not of their hunting companions, but of their quarry: the horns of gazelle and ibex (Fig. 44). Interestingly, among peoples who practise shamanism the world over, horns have a common significance. They are regarded as symbols of regrowth and therefore rebirth. As we shall see, much of the Eastern Desert rock art may have had a funerary purpose. We should not, therefore, exclude the possibility that the ibex itself – as possessor of the most impressive horns on the savannah – may have had a special significance to prehistoric Egyptians, connected with the afterlife. This might account for its frequency in Predynastic rock art. On another level, people clearly believed that donning the most distinctive part of the animal they were pursuing helped to give them a better chance in the hunt. It might even tip the balance in favour of the hunter by giving him animal as well as human qualities.

This ancient practice of invoking magical powers by wearing animal attributes was not confined to humans. The artists of prehistoric Egypt also seem to have imagined their gods in a similar way. Deities could take the form of animals – for example, the soaring falcon overhead being the embodiment of the sky god – but they could also take human form, in which case they were distinguished from mere mortals by their superhuman size and their animal accessories. And so it is that the earliest certain depiction of an anthropomorphic deity in Egyptian art – our cattle-controller from the Wadi Umm Salam – wears the characteristic twin plumes of divinity.

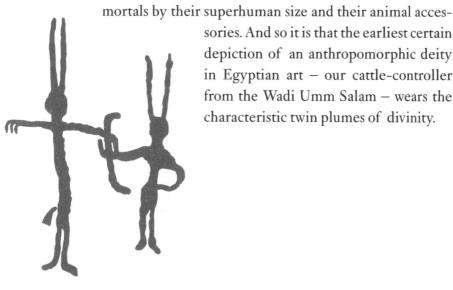

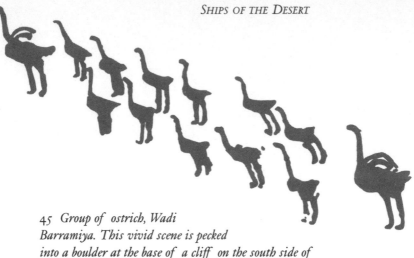

*45 Group of ostrich, Wadi
Barramiya. This vivid scene is pecked
into a boulder at the base of a cliff on the south side of
the wadi. It illustrates not only the prehistoric fauna of the eastern savannah, but also
the fascination of Egyptian artists for the animal world.*

*46 OPPOSITE Carved ivory comb decorated with rows of animals. The depiction of
ordered rows of wild animals was a metaphor for the imposition of control over the
unruly forces of nature. It was a favourite motif in late prehistoric art, but its roots go
back much further.*

In later Egyptian art, when worn by such gods as Amun-Ra, these
plumes are clearly identifiable as ostrich feathers. It is very likely that
this was also their origin. Ostriches loom large in the rock art of the
Eastern Desert. There is scarcely a hunting scene that does not include
at least one bird. In several locations, including the Wadi Umm Salam,
whole families of ostrich are shown. One particularly striking example
occurs on a fallen boulder at the foot of a cliff in the Wadi Barramiya.
Here, the prehistoric artist has taken great care to peck into the rock a
group of no fewer than thirteen ostriches (Fig. 45). The eleven smaller
birds are protected by an adult at each end. For the prehistoric inhabitants of Egypt, ostriches must indeed have been awesome creatures.
Their size and speed made them formidable quarry. It is no wonder that
on one early decorated palette, a group of ostriches is shown being
confronted by a hunter (or possibly a shaman) wearing an ostrich mask
(see Fig. 29). How the hunters of prehistoric Egypt must have wished
for the qualities of the ostrich! How natural that they should conceive

of their gods possessing just these powers; and how appropriate that they should identify their deities in art by placing on their heads a pair of ostrich plumes.

The neat row of ostriches mentioned above exemplifies another deep strand of belief in Egyptian religion: the idea that the chaotic natural world could be ordered – as well as dominated – through the magical power of art. It was not always necessary to show wild animals being hunted or felled. Sometimes, the same purpose could be served by showing usually unruly wild animals in neat, ordered rows. The contrast between the orderly composition and the chaos it had sup-planted was a powerful metaphor in its own right. Some of the most famous examples of this motif are found on carved ivory combs and knife-handles, produced by expert craftsmen in the royal workshops of late Predynastic Upper Egypt (Fig. 46). The decoration typically com-prises several different kinds of wild animals. The most elaborate knife-handle, now in the Brooklyn Museum, shows an extraordinary variety of fauna, including elephant, giraffe, ibex and ratel (honey-badger), demonstrating the Egyptians' detailed knowledge of the natural world. An earlier example of deliberately ordered animals was found in the Painted Tomb at Nekhen. In addition to the famous procession of boats – which we will return to later in this chapter – the decorative scheme included a huge variety of other vignettes, many of which were to become standard elements of ancient Egyptian iconography (see Fig. 12). One shows a line of three captive ibex, arranged on a

horizontal line. While this is probably the earliest example of the so-called 'base line' in ancient Egyptian art, the idea of a neatly ordered row of ibex goes back much further, to the rock art of 4000 BC: a cliff on the southern side of the Wadi Umm Salam bears a remarkably similar scene, only this time the ibex number more than half a dozen (four are shown in Fig. 47).

All the scenes discussed so far – from tethered cattle, to hunting, to neatly ordered rows of wild animals – reflect the most fundamental belief in ancient Egyptian religion: the constant struggle between created order (symbolized by humans, aided by the gods) and chaos (symbolized by the untamed natural world, and especially wild animals). At two sites in the Eastern Desert, this conflict assumes its ultimate expression in the ritual slaughter of a captured animal by a human hunter. In the Wadi Abu Wasil, the animal in question is an

47 *Four animals from a row of ibex, Wadi Umm Salam. This is an early example of the motif which symbolized the triumph of order over chaos. It pre-figures a strikingly similar scene in the famous Painted Tomb at Nekhen.*

48 OPPOSITE ABOVE *Ritual slaughter of an antelope, Wadi Abu Wasil. This dramatic scene, like its counterpart in the Wadi Mineh (Figure 49) was probably intended to guarantee, by assertion, the dominance of humans over the threatening natural world that surrounded them out on the savannah.*

49, 50 OPPOSITE BELOW *Ritual slaughter of an ostrich, Wadi Mineh (left). This dramatic scene of human dominance over the natural world is strikingly paralleled by the decoration of Tutankhamun's ostrich-feather fan, from 2,500 years later (right). Such parallels demonstrate the longevity, and great antiquity, of Egyptian civilization.*

unidentified quadruped, probably an antelope of some kind (Fig. 48).
At a major rock art site in the Wadi Mineh, the sacrificial victim is an
ostrich, that most eloquent symbol of animal power (Fig. 49). In both
cases, the captured animal is shown tethered to a large rock, with no
hope of escape. The hunter dispatches the victim at close range with
his bow and arrow. In many ways, this faintly disturbing symbolism
foreshadows the classic image of ancient Egyptian kingship: the king
beating out the brains of his captive enemy, who is kneeling before him,
with a mace. It is also comparable to the famous bull-hunting scene in
the mortuary temple of Ramesses III at Medinet Habu. Here, the king
in his chariot, spears a huge wild bull which has become entangled in a
papyrus thicket with no hope of escape. In such circumstances, the

defeat of chaos was an imperative that overruled any thoughts of mercy. For the Egyptians, there could be no let-up in the eternal battle to preserve order. The magical power of art was one of the most effective weapons in this battle, and was deployed ruthlessly from prehistoric times until the collapse of ancient Egyptian civilization.

So much for the scenes of herding and hunting in the Eastern Desert. What about the other major category of rock art? If the animal scenes are to be interpreted in terms of ancient Egyptian religion, could the same also be true of the boats? A final type of wild animal that we have not yet discussed may, quite literally, point the way. The huge decorated rock wall near the 'jacuzzi' in the Wadi Umm Salam is dominated by the figures of three towering giraffes. They are particularly distinctive in the stylized depiction of their tails, shown with four greatly elongated hairs that nearly reach to the ground. What are these animals doing, somehow controlling the whole composition? In common with other ancient cultures, the Egyptians believed giraffes to be harbingers of the future. Their sheer height put them in closer touch with the heavens than any other ground-dweller. From such a vantage point, they could see further into the distance than any other land animal. Little wonder that in hieroglyphic writing the giraffe was used for the verb 'to foretell'. It is likely that this attribute – the ability to see into the distance, to bridge the present and the future – explains the importance of giraffes in prehistoric Egyptian art. Their presence in the Wadi Umm Salam transforms the significance of the entire tableau over which they gaze. It was not intended as a recollection of things that had happened, but as a foretelling of what would happen. The forces conjured in the art do not, primarily, belong to this world, but to the spirit world. Their power extends from the here and now to the hereafter.

At the lower right-hand corner of the wall an ancient artist has lovingly drawn a boat, its many oars stretching down at an angle as it travels. What cargo does this boat carry, and where is it going? More than the many fascinating images of hunting and herding, it is the boat drawings that have excited the most interest and debate among scholars and amateurs alike. Without doubt, they are the most striking feature of the Eastern Desert rock art, especially as they are found hundreds of miles from the nearest water (the Nile to the west and the Red Sea to the east). Interpretations of their symbolism and significance have varied widely in the century since they were first encountered by Western explorers.

Although Arthur Weigall was the first Egyptologist to publish large numbers of the boat drawings, he seems to have shown little interest in trying to unlock their meaning. It was Winkler who really set the debate alight with his radical interpretation that they recorded 'Eastern Invaders', a 'master race' who had come from the east to bring civilization to Egypt in prehistoric times. Noticing a passing resemblance between some of the high-prowed boats in the Eastern Desert with similar vessels on Mesopotamian seals (from a thousand years later – although Winkler did not know this), he argued that the ancient Mesopotamians had sailed to Egypt's Red Sea coast, then journeyed through the desert wadis to enter the Nile Valley from the east, leaving their marks on the rocks as they went.

Even after the Second World War, the theory that ancient Egyptian civilization had been the creation of a 'master race' clung on in some quarters of Egyptology. Archaeologists as eminent as Bryan Emery could still write, as late as 1961: 'towards the close of the fourth millennium BC we find… a civilized aristocracy or master race ruling over the whole of Egypt.' In support of the theory, Emery cited the apparent sudden appearance of the hallmarks of Egyptian civilization towards the end of the prehistoric period. Predynastic archaeology was still in its infancy, and it would be another fifteen years before excavations began to reveal the ancient, indigenous roots of Egyptian civilization. Emery also pointed to the Mesopotamian iconography and architecture characteristic of Egyptian elite culture at the end of the fourth millennium BC. Once again, archaeologists were only just beginning to be able to date prehistoric material. Emery was not to know that his evidence for contacts between Egypt and Mesopotamia belonged to a period some 500 to 1,000 years later than the ships of the Eastern Desert.

Most recently, the 'dynastic race' theory has been championed by David Rohl. Following on from Winkler, and especially Emery, Rohl suggested that the boat petroglyphs of the Eastern Desert were made, not by the alleged 'Eastern Invaders' themselves, but by the local inhabitants who observed them as they dragged their great warships along the wadis from the Red Sea. It is certainly an incredible and enchanting theory, with considerable popular appeal. However, it is not supported by the evidence from Egypt or Mesopotamia. Amongst other flaws, it conveniently ignores (as did Winkler) the presence of boat drawings in the Western Desert, and also the fundamental purpose of Egyptian art at all periods – which was to perpetuate an idealized view of the cosmos, and to explore the interaction between the human, natural and supernatural worlds, not to record everyday occurrences.

If the boats do not, then, depict real craft, carrying invaders to Egypt, what is their true significance? If we examine the role of boats in pharaonic art and culture, we begin to find some clues. In the tombs of high officials, from the Old Kingdom onwards, boats are most frequently encountered in scenes showing hunting in the marshes. While important individuals may well have indulged in this pastime, the purpose of the tomb scenes – as we have already noted – was primarily religious. Laden with symbolism of rebirth and resurrection, the marsh hunting scene was designed to help the deceased tomb-owner to be born again into the afterlife. In private tombs of the Middle Kingdom, the body of the owner is shown being transported by boat to Abydos, in a symbolic pilgrimage to the cult centre of Osiris, god of the underworld. This same theme is also found in the wooden tomb models of the period, where the deceased is usually shown laid out under an awning in the middle of the boat. One of the earliest model boats from Egypt, a pottery example from a Predynastic tomb, indicates an association of boats with the afterlife journey from earliest times.

This idea that the dead embarked on a journey by boat is echoed, in a royal setting, in the earliest religious texts to survive from ancient Egypt, the Pyramid Texts. Inscribed in the underground chambers of royal pyramids from the end of the Fifth Dynasty to the end of the

Sixth, the Pyramid Texts comprise an elaborate and complex series of spells and incantations. They were designed – once again – to ensure that the spirit of the deceased would reach the afterlife successfully, overcoming all the dangers and obstacles in its way. The texts describe different ways of reaching the afterlife (which was believed to take place in the starry sky); but boats are perhaps the most common. After all, the boat was the primary form of transport in Egypt, where the main artery of communication was the River Nile. It was only natural that the best way of reaching and crossing the watery firmament of heaven should also be by boat. For this reason, royal interments from the First Dynasty to the end of the Pyramid Age were often accompanied by boat burials. King Khasekhemwy, buried at Abydos at the end of the Second Dynasty, was provided with a fleet of twelve cedar-wood boats, to assist his journey into the next world. Khufu, the builder of the Great Pyramid, had two huge boats buried next to his pyramid in stone-cut pits. One of them now stands in a purpose-built museum, testifying to the boat-building skills of the ancient Egyptians and the force of their belief in the afterlife journey by boat.

A thousand years after Khufu built his Great Pyramid, Egypt's rulers were interred, not under man-made mountains of stone, but in great tombs, hewn into the rock in the Valley of the Kings. In these tombs, too, there is a preponderance of boat imagery. It is in a boat that the dead king is dragged down to the underworld, to join Osiris. When the sun god Ra passes through the night regions and joins with Osiris, the king's spirit is re-awakened to accompany Ra in his everlasting cosmic journey – by boat. The solar bark of Ra was the most important boat in Egyptian religion. It was known as the 'boat of millions', referring to the multitude of spirits that joined the sun god in his unending cycle. Every additional spirit that joined the boat bolstered the crew and lent extra support to Ra in his daily battle with chaos, represented by the serpent Apep. In their funerary beliefs as in their world-view, the Egyptians placed the battle between good and evil in pole position. Interestingly, in several royal tombs of the New Kingdom, the solar bark of Ra, with the king aboard, is shown being dragged through the underworld by willing helpers (Plate 22), until it can be re-launched (Plate 20) into the watery firmament of heaven at the place where earth and heaven meet, the eastern horizon.

Once safely back in the sky, the solar bark carries Ra and his helpers through the heavens. The belief that the gods travelled by boat was an ancient one in Egyptian religion. During the great religious festivals of the New Kingdom, images of the gods would be carried in boat shrines from temple to temple. Nearly 2,000 years earlier, at the beginning of the First Dynasty, the same belief was expressed in the decoration of an ivory comb, made for the tomb of a king. It shows the sky god, in the form of a falcon, travelling in a boat over the vault of heaven, which is represented as the outspread wings of a vulture. Just as boats were the principal form of transport for humans in ancient Egypt, so they were also believed to be the main mode of transport for the gods.

Boats for the afterlife journey, boats for the gods: could it be that the boats of the Eastern Desert rock art have the same symbolism? The largest and probably the most impressive of all boat petroglyphs is pecked into the smooth surface of the rock face on the north side of the Wadi Abu Wasil (Plates 11 and 19). Unlike many other sites of rock art, this particular one catches the full force of the sun throughout much of the day. It seems that it was deliberately sited to be as visible and as conspicuous as possible. The boat contains two larger figures with twin plumed head-dresses and, between them and at either side, three smaller figures of similar appearance. The scale of this scene, and the distinctive attributes of the boat's five occupants, strongly

51 ABOVE *Boat with man and ostrich, Wadi Abu Wasil. This curious scene is difficult to interpret, but it is likely that the ostrich represents a deity or supernatural spirit. Ostriches seem to have played an important role in prehistoric ritual and religion, perhaps because of their impressive size and speed (compare Figure 29).*

52 BELOW *Cow being dragged in a boat, Wadi Barramiya. A strikingly similar scene to this appears in the temple of Hatshepsut, a pharaoh of the New Kingdom, some twenty-five centuries later. Eastern Desert rock art reveals the origins of many of the familiar themes from ancient Egyptian art and religion.*

suggest that they are deities. Nearby, on another rock face exposed to
the sun, are further boats with strange, spiky-haired passengers. While
the original purpose of such drawings may never be known, it seems
very likely that they depict gods, or at least supernatural spirits. Even
more plausible candidates for divine boats are those which carry the
representation of a larger-than-life animal. An isolated rock drawing
in a tributary valley of the Wadi Abu Wasil shows a boat, covered by an
awning, bearing the twin figures of a man and a large ostrich. Significantly, perhaps, the ostrich stands at the prow of the boat, in front of
the human occupant (Fig. 51). Given the religious connotations of
ostriches, discussed above, it seems very likely that this particular bird
represents a deity. Also of divine stature is the cow or bull which is
shown being dragged in a boat by a crew of human helpers in a petroglyph in the Wadi Barramiya (Fig. 52). It calls to mind a very similar
scene in the Eighteenth Dynasty temple of the female king Hatshepsut
at Deir el-Bahri. This shows the mother goddess Hathor, in the form of
a cow, being dragged in her divine boat. We know that cattle played an

absolutely central role in the lives and livelihoods of prehistoric Egyptians. Little wonder, then, that people may have worshipped one of their deities or supernatural spirits in bovine form.

Just around the corner from this cattle deity in the Wadi Barramiya lies one of the most moving images in the Eastern Desert: a large, flat-bottomed boat with squared ends, containing a central cabin, fifty stick-like figures (presumably the boat's occupants) and, at the back of the boat, a superhuman figure wearing twin plumes, extending one arm horizontally over the heads of the crew towards the prow (Fig. 53; see also Plate 23). It is difficult to interpret the large figure as anything other than a god. He seems to command the ship, and its occupants. He is also, very clearly, pointing the way – but to where? At the most basic, he points in the direction of travel. This may be all that the artist intended: to show that the god commanded the boat. There is, however, another, tantalizing possibility. The scene is carved inside a shaded rock-shelter, on the south side of the Wadi Barramiya. In pointing to the right, the figure thus gestures towards the west, land of the dead in

53 Boat with plumed figure, Wadi Barramiya. The pointing figure is almost certainly a god, gesturing towards the west, the traditional land of the dead in ancient Egyptian religion. The theme of a journey by boat remained central to Egyptian concepts of the afterlife.

54 OPPOSITE Funerary boat, Kanais. The upraised arms of the figures may be a gesture of mourning, while the curious projections from the central cabin are probably the feet of the corpses that are being taken on their final journey.

Egyptian mythology. Could it be that this boat is embarking on a journey to the afterlife, the crew (perhaps transfigured spirits) watched over by a presiding deity? A curious, and as yet unidentified feature of this boat is the object inside the central cabin. It looks rather like a bird, raising its wings for flight. But it could just as easily be a flame, or any other object for that matter. From much later parallels, it seems most likely to represent the corpse, or spirit, of a dead person. Such an interpretation would certainly fit with what we know about Egyptian funerary beliefs. Luckily, at some other rock art sites in the same wadi, the contents of ships' cabins are more easily identified. At a dramatic cliff face on the sheer northern side of the Wadi Barramiya, a veritable flotilla of boats adorns the rock surface. One vessel contains four large figures, each wearing a single plume. They stand in pairs, either side of the central cabin containing a crude stick-like human figure. In this case, there can be little doubt that the boat is carrying human cargo. Another concentration of boats lies further to the west, near the New Kingdom rock-cut temple at Kanais. Particularly distinctive is the vessel with a cabin shaped like a quarter-circle. From the vertical opening jut four curious objects resembling golf-clubs (Fig. 54). In fact, they are probably pairs of feet, belonging to two corpses laid out in the cabin and covered from view. Here again, the boat appears to be ferrying the dead.

As far as identifying the cargo is concerned, the clearest example of all is also the most beautifully executed boat petroglyph yet discovered in the Eastern Desert. It lies on the south side of a remote dry valley,

the Wadi el-Atwani. Nearby, high in the cliff face, is a deep cave which may have held important religious connotations for the prehistoric people. The boat itself is decorated with a bull-standard at the stern, and twin fronds at the prow. A crew of seventeen mans the oars to propel the craft forwards. At the stern, as in the Wadi Barramiya example, a large figure points in the direction of travel, over the heads of the other occupants (Fig. 55). Once again, the orientation of the drawing means that he points towards the west. In this boat, however, there is no central cabin. Instead, the principal occupant (other than the pointing figure) is a human figure standing near the prow. The scenes in the Valley of the Kings royal tombs spring immediately to mind: a divine boat, presided over by a god, ferrying the reborn king to the afterlife. While the passenger in the Wadi el-Atwani may not be a king, there is little doubt that the boat is carrying him into another dimension, with divine assistance.

55 Boat with pointing figure, Wadi el-Atwani. Situated at the foot of a cave that may have been the location for religious rituals, this beautifully executed scene is one of the finest in the Eastern Desert. Like its counterpart in the Wadi Barramiya (Figure 53), it may represent the journey of deceased souls into the afterlife.

56 OPPOSITE Prehistoric figurines with upraised arms. Such figurines were quite commonly interred in graves, perhaps as a mark of mourning (compare Figure 54). An alternative explanation is that the arms mimic bulls' horns, conveying the deep and complex spiritual relationship that existed between humans and cattle in prehistoric times.

Further evidence to support a funerary interpretation of the desert boats is provided by the accompanying figures in many scenes. For example, the 'golf club' boat at Kanais, mentioned above, bears – in addition to the cabin and its contents – three human figures, each with upraised, curved arms. Figures in exactly the same posture are found throughout the Eastern Desert, nearly always in connection with boats. Particularly good examples can be seen in the eastern Wadi Barramiya (Plate 18) and at sites on the northern side of the Wadi Hammamat. Very similar figures also occur in three dimensions, as small clay figurines found in Predynastic graves. The same posture is also commonly shown on the decorated pottery of the Nagada II period. Whilst not exclusively funerary, it is notable that this particular type of painted pottery is much rarer in settlements than in cemeteries; so it may have been manufactured principally for burial. If human figures with upraised arms occur so frequently in funerary contexts throughout the prehistoric period, what is the significance of the posture itself? Such figures were dubbed 'dancing goddesses' by early Egyptologists, and it has been suggested that the gesture of curving the arms above the head mimicked the horns of cattle. People shown in this manner may, therefore, have been taking part in a ritual 'cow dance' (Fig. 56). This would fit well with what we know about the central importance of cattle in the culture of early Predynastic Egypt. However, there is another, perhaps connected, interpretation of the upraised-arms posture: that it may have represented an attitude of mourning. This would certainly account for the preponderance of such figures on funerary pottery, among funerary figurines, and in the scenes of boats in the Eastern Desert.

If many of the boats do, therefore, depict the afterlife journey, can we tell what sort of destination, what sort of afterlife, the Predynastic Egyptians envisaged for their departed kinsmen and, indeed, for themselves? The Pyramid Texts, although only written down in the late Fifth and Sixth Dynasties, may well date back to an earlier period. It is even possible – although difficult to prove – that some were first formulated at the very beginning of Egyptian history, in the First Dynasty. One of the most striking categories of text has been called 'transformation texts'. They deal with the transformation of the dead king and his resurrection into the afterlife. They often describe, among other things, the particular means by which the king will make the journey from the tomb (the pyramid) into the hereafter. The pyramid itself played an important role in this transformation, since on one level it was designed to resemble the rays of the sun; on another level it served as a giant staircase: both are means of ascent referred to in the Pyramid Texts. Interestingly, boats are the most common method of transport used by the dead king to ascend to the heavens. This is not surprising in a land dominated by the River Nile, and it helps to explain the ancient practice of burying boats with the deceased, whether in miniature form (as tomb models), or life-sized craft. The boat buried adjacent to the tomb of a royal prince at North Saqqara at the beginning of the First Dynasty; the two boats provided for a high government official at Abu Rawash in the middle of the dynasty; the fleet of twelve boats buried at Abydos next to the funerary palace of King Khasekhemwy at the end of the Second Dynasty; and the two great cedar barks buried next to the Great Pyramid of Khufu at Giza: these were all designed to help the dead person reach the afterlife as efficiently as possible.

As far as the afterlife itself was concerned, the loftiness of the pyramids hints at its celestial dimension. The Pyramid Texts refer to a journey in the company of the sun and stars. In particular, the king was believed to join the circumpolar stars which surround the Pole Star. Because they never disappear from view (unlike other stars which 'rise and set') when observed from the northern hemisphere, the ancient Egyptians called them 'the Indestructibles' and believed them to be the ultimate destination of the king's spirit after death. By joining the circumpolar stars, the king could be absorbed into the great, unending rhythm of the cosmos. Ordinary mortals, too, might hope to share in such an afterlife. The Egyptians called the night sky 'a thousand are her souls', expressing the belief that each star was the transfigured soul of a dead person. This, then, was the pattern for the afterlife that Egyptians believed in at the time of the pyramids. Could it also have been the belief of those who left images on the rocks of the eastern savannah some 1,500 years earlier?

One of the most remote boat drawings suggests the answer to this question may be yes. It is pecked into the smooth rock face on the northern side of the Wadi Abu Mu'awwad, a narrow and winding valley in the very heart of the Eastern Desert. The site is a dramatic one, located at one of the sharpest bends in the wadi. From the high desert on top of the cliff, there is a fantastic view over the surrounding terrain. However, there is nothing particularly remarkable about the boat drawing itself. What is more striking is the small detail which has been added some distance above the prow: a star. The technique and patination of the star and boat are identical, suggesting that both were made at the same time, as part of the same composition. It looks very much as if the boat is following the star.

A second, even clearer example, has been lovingly drawn at the back of a rock-shelter on the northern side of the Wadi Hammamat. This particular rock art site (Winkler's Site 5) would have been passed by anyone striking out from the cultivation towards the siltstone quarries of the Black Mountains. The rock-shelter, at the northern end of a line of bluffs, has an abundance of boats in a very small area, indicating that it must have held a special significance for the prehistoric people who passed this way. The most impressive boat, and the largest, measures some 24 inches (60 centimetres) long. There is a central cabin, containing two rows of people, probably dead. The boat is dominated by a single large figure, its arms curved upwards in the familiar gesture of mourning. Hovering above the prow of the boat is a carefully drawn six-pointed star (see Plate 9). Here, and in the Wadi Abu Mu'awwad, there seems to have been no doubt in the minds of the ancient artists that the afterlife journey would be guided by a star. Whether or not the stars were also believed to be the boat's ultimate destination, we can only guess; but it is a tempting possibility.

The concentration of boat drawings found at Site 5 is mirrored elsewhere in the Eastern Desert. The main part of Site 26 on the northern side of the Wadi Abu Wasil preserves a remarkable collection of boats, as do some rather more secluded sites in the neighbouring Wadi Mineh. The cliff face at Kanais is literally covered in boats of various shapes and sizes. But perhaps the most remarkable armada of all lies high up on the northern side of the Wadi Barramiya, directly opposite the entrance to the Wadi Umm Hajalij (where abundant rock art is also to be found). Some 100 feet (30 metres) above the wadi floor, a long horizontal strip of the smooth cliff face is covered with a procession of fifteen boats (see Plate 15). What is the significance of these great flotillas? Boat processions are not uncommon in Egyptian art (Plate 17). The main scene in the Painted Tomb at Nekhen showed a procession of boats, one of them containing the image of the prehistoric ruler for whom the tomb was made. The painted linen cloth from an earlier ruler's grave at Gebelein shows a similar gathering of boats (see Plate 12). In both cases, the convoy of craft seems to have had particular mortuary connotations, perhaps recalling the funeral ceremony itself.

This symbolism may also account for some of the groups of boats in the Eastern Desert. However, it is also quite likely that some of the desert armadas were created over long periods of time, perhaps many centuries. At the most important sites, each new generation may have added its own boat to the expanding tableau – much like Aboriginal rock art sites in northern Australia which saw continuous use over thousands of years. In this case, the sites concerned probably held a special spiritual significance for the communities that visited them.

They may have been revered as gateways to the next world, or places where the divide between the natural and supernatural worlds was unusually narrow. Such places are known the world over. Again in Australia, certain landmarks (such as Uluru – 'Ayers Rock') are still believed to hold special religious significance for the indigenous people. Even in the 'modern' Western world, churches are often found to have been built on the sites of earlier, pre-Christian places of worship. The spiritual associations of specific localities, once established, are surprisingly long-lasting. We can easily imagine some of the more dramatic locations in the Eastern Desert having held such associations for the prehistoric Egyptians. It is not too fanciful to suggest that some of the concentrations of rock art are the prehistoric equivalent of the great Egyptian temples: places where generation upon generation of humans might call upon divine assistance in the trials of life.

Visits to such places would have been particularly important at moments of stress. The build-up to a hunting expedition, with all its associated dangers, would have been one kind of occasion on which recourse to divine intervention – or at least magical assistance – was desirable. The uncertainties of a hunt would have been as nothing compared to the uncertainties of what lay beyond the grave. Questions about the meaning of life are brought into the sharpest focus by a death. Since the very beginning of the human species, a death in the family or social group has been accompanied by rituals – intended as much for the continued wellbeing of the survivors and for the welfare of the deceased. From the decorated tombs of the nobles at Thebes to the great pyramids of Giza, death and funerary concerns inspired the most dazzling and enduring monuments of ancient Egypt. Given everything we know about the boats of the Eastern Desert and their symbolism, it seems very likely that the major sites of this art were also funerary in nature. They may therefore have served as permanent cenotaphs, rather like the giant barrows of Bronze Age England. Perhaps each new boat added to a site commemorated another death – giving visual expression to the hopes and beliefs of those left behind for the eternal future of their departed companion.

This raises another intriguing possibility: perhaps the various rock art sites throughout the Eastern Desert belonged to different tribal groups, different communities. Once again, the funerary monuments of Bronze Age Britain may provide a parallel: although their practical purpose was as burials for the dead, they were just as important as territorial markers for the living. This helps to explain their visibility in the landscape, for each barrow proclaimed: 'this is where our ancestors are buried; this is our land.' As far as the cattle-herders of Predynastic Egypt are concerned, we simply do not know how far they wandered in search of new grazing after the summer rains. Did they stick to the grasslands closest to their particular stretch of the Nile Valley, or did they venture further afield? It is very likely that each community had a favoured area to which it returned year after year, probably following well-worn routes through the winding wadis. In this case, the wonderful collections of rock art in the Wadi Barramiya were probably made by a community from the southern part of the Nile Valley, in the vicinity of Nekheb (modern Elkab). By contrast, those in the Wadi Umm Salam and Wadi Abu Wasil were probably the creations of entirely different communities; while the art of the Wadi Hammamat may have been made by people whose valley homes were in the vicinity of modern Guft. It is certainly noticeable, even to the casual observer, that particular artistic traditions seem to characterize particular wadis. For example, squarish, flat-bottomed boats predominate in the Wadi Abu Wasil; whereas more elaborate, sickle-shaped craft are more common in the western Wadi Barramiya. Much more work needs to be done, analysing the abundant rock art of the Eastern Desert, to see if distinct patterns emerge. The political groupings of prehistoric Egypt are usually reconstructed from the distribution of cemeteries in the Nile Valley. Perhaps the rock art of the Eastern Desert holds another key to unlocking the pattern of power in Egypt's distant past, centuries before the emergence of a unified state.

~ · ~ · ~

*L*ike the shadowy figure with outstretched arm in the Wadi el-Atwani, the ships of the desert pose more questions than they answer. They are perhaps the most surprising aspect of the rock art, and certainly the most intriguing. They bring us face-to-face with the most powerful fears and emotions of their creators, who lived some 6,000 years ago. They allow us a brief glimpse into the lives – and deaths – of Egypt's early inhabitants. Yet, curiously, the concerns that seem to loom large in the art, and the picture that emerges of life in 4000 BC, are not as strange as we might have expected. In fact, they are surprisingly familiar. This is because, like our shadowy figure, the Eastern Desert rock art points the way: to the emergence of classic ancient Egyptian civilization a thousand years later.

That familiar Egypt, the Egypt of gods and tombs, did not emerge overnight. It was nurtured and developed gradually, over centuries. Egyptologists have realized this for many years now. But in attempting to chart the birth of ancient Egypt, have they been looking for the cradle of civilization in the wrong place? That is the question for the final chapter.

6

CRADLE OF CIVILIZATION
Re-thinking Ancient Egyptian Origins

Egypt is the gift of the Nile. So said Herodotus, the Greek historian, when he visited the land of the pharaohs in the fifth century BC; and any visitor to Egypt today would have to agree. The river cuts a narrow swathe of green through dry, inhospitable desert. In some places the floodplain is less than half a mile wide, the cultivable land occupying an impossibly restricted strip between riverbank and desert edge. Until the very recent development of large irrigation projects in the Sinai and the Western Desert, all of Egypt's agricultural production was concentrated in the Nile Valley. So too was the vast majority of its burgeoning population. The River Nile still provides water for drinking, washing, bathing and irrigation to the millions of people who live along its banks. Even in the era of modern, metalled roads, the river is still, in many ways, the country's main artery of communication. Egypt would, indeed, be unthinkable without the Nile.

But it was not always so. In far-off times before the beginning of recorded history, the climate was very different from today's. Rain fell on a seasonal basis over large parts of southern Egypt. Today's deserts were dry grasslands, transformed by the annual rains into attractive grazing for herds of wild and domesticated animals alike. In this prehistoric period, large numbers of people lived in what is now desert –

not only lived but thrived. They left their marks everywhere on the rocks, as petroglyphs: pecked or incised images of those things that most concerned them, reflections of their deepest beliefs, insights into their own view of the world. So, which of these two very different environments – fertile Nile Valley or semi-arid savannah – can lay claim to be the cradle of ancient Egyptian civilization?

For most Egyptologists and writers up to the present day, there has been little doubt. The capital city of Egypt has, since the beginning of history, stood next to the Nile at the point where the river begins to divide, forming the wide expanse of the Delta. Cairo and before it the ancient city of Memphis are both distinctively riverine settlements. They are port cities, even though located hundreds of miles inland. Their economies have depended upon bustling harbours, upon their control of river traffic. From the time of the first pharaohs, through the Roman Empire to the present day, Egypt's wealth has been inextricably linked to its agricultural potential. It was, after all, the 'bread basket' of the Roman world. The prodigious fertility of the Egyptian soil depends entirely on the River Nile. Not only does the river provide water to irrigate the crops; but, until the building of the Aswan High Dam in the 1960s, the annual flood also covered the fields with a layer of fine silt, renewing the fertility of the land every year. Surely it was this agricultural productivity that formed the basis for the development of one of the world's greatest civilizations?

Comparisons with other great civilizations of the ancient world seemed to confirm the central importance of the river in the process of cultural development. The Tigris and Euphrates, the Indus, the Yangtze: all gave their surrounding regions a head start, all became centres of great cultures. Why should this be so? According to the prevailing line of argument, the daily struggle for survival in lands where subsistence is difficult stifles cultural creativity. If you have to spend most of your day just looking for your next meal, you are hardly likely to have the time or energy to develop arts and crafts, or to sit and think. By contrast, if all you have to do to feed your family is plant some seeds, then sit back and watch the crops grow tall as they are fed and watered by the natural regime of a benign river – then you may well have time on your hands, time to progress beyond the mundane struggles of survival into something deeper, richer, more imaginative. Surely it could be no coincidence that the earliest, prehistoric antecedent of classic ancient Egyptian civilization – the Predynastic Badarian culture – arose at the same time that farming was introduced to the Nile Valley? When Egyptians became farmers, they planted a seed that was to grow and mature into pharaonic civilization. Like the Mesopotamians and Chinese, when freed from the daily search for food, the ancient Egyptians were able to devote their energies to other activities. The particularly favourable annual regime of the Nile would explain why the Egyptians were among the first to develop a sophisticated culture, including painting, sculpture, monumental architecture, writing, elaborate religious and political ideologies. Or would it?

~ · ~ · ~

Deep in the Sahara desert, in the far south of Egypt, not far from the Sudanese border, an American team of archaeologists excavating a remote site in 1992 made a startling discovery. At first the small circle of rough stones laid out on the desert surface looked unremarkable. Then, on closer inspection, the true wonder of what they had found began to dawn. Four pairs of stones were somewhat larger, and set closer together than their companions. A quick check with a pocket compass was all that was needed to reveal their purpose. Two of the pairs of larger stones faced each other across the circle, on a line that ran precisely north–south. The other two pairs were aligned to 62 degrees east of north – pointing to the position of the sunrise on 21 June, the summer solstice. This remarkable monument was, in fact, Egypt's Stonehenge, a stone calendar designed and built to measure time and, in particular, signal the beginning of summer. How old was this amazing construction, what people had built it, and why? Fortunately, the excavations at the site – called Nabta Playa – had been going on for nearly twenty years when the astronomical stone circle was discovered. Egyptologists already knew a great deal about the ancient inhabitants of Nabta, their lifestyle, and why predicting the onset of summer would have been so important to them.

It is curious that a site as important as Nabta should be so little known, even among Egyptologists. Here, on the shores of a temporary lake (or 'playa') that last dried up long, long ago, prehistoric people created a truly remarkable society. Occupation of the site seems to have begun almost as soon as the climate made the region inhabitable year-round, perhaps as early as 8000 BC. The peak of human activity coincided with the wettest climatic phase, lasting for about a thousand years from 5000 to 4000 BC. The people of Nabta cultivated barley, but their main source of subsistence was cattle. Indeed, they may have been some of the very earliest people in the whole of Africa to practise cattle-herding as a way of life. The age of the cattle bones found at the site, combined with their relative rarity, indicates that the Nabta people kept herds for their renewable by-products, milk and blood, rather than their meat. But life was by no means easy. These people lived life on the edge. The environment was harsh and unforgiving. If the people relied on their cattle, the cattle relied on water – a commodity in short supply. Crucial to the whole viability of the cattle-herders' way of life was the advent of the rainy season. This began each year at the start of the summer, transforming the shallow depression around which they lived into a lake. This in turn provided sufficient moisture to support grassland and the pasture that the herds so badly needed. If the summer rains came late, the grass would not grow, and the cattle and people would die. No wonder they built an astronomical clock to predict the first day of summer: their entire existence depended on it. As the previous summer's fodder began to run out, they must have calculated how much longer they needed to eke out their dwindling supplies before fresh rain brought new life.

Not surprisingly, the people at Nabta Playa celebrated the arrival of the rainy season with major festivities. Large numbers of cattle bones found in particular locations suggest that the ritual slaughter of cattle played an important part in these celebrations. Since cattle were highly valued, and rarely used for meat, killing them is likely to have been an event laden with religious meaning. At this most crucial turning-point of the year, a communal feast with beef on the menu may well have been part of the festivities – just as the mid-winter, Yuletide feast, which has long marked the turning point of the year for northern European cultures, has traditionally featured delicacies rarely consumed at other times. But there was more to the killing of precious cattle than providing meat. It may well be that the animals selected for slaughter were offered as sacrifices, to thank the supernatural powers that controlled the rains. The edge of one of the major wadis running into the Nabta Playa depression is lined with burials of cattle, each covered with large stones. These bear all the hallmarks of high-status graves, and they confirm the overriding importance of cattle in Nabta culture.

It was not just cattle that were accorded special status in Nabta society. To survive in this precarious and stressful environment, the prehistoric inhabitants needed a structured society, one in which roles were clearly demarcated and understood. They also needed wise individuals who could make the critical decisions upon which the entire community's welfare depended. In other words, they needed experienced rulers. This has been one of the most startling revelations of the Nabta Playa excavations: that a cattle-herding, pastoralist people were by no means primitive nomads. Rather, they developed a surprisingly advanced culture that paved the way for ancient Egyptian civilization. We have no evidence for how the rulers of Nabta were chosen. There is no indication that authority had yet become hereditary, so perhaps leaders were selected on the basis of their wisdom and experience. While the mechanism for acquiring power may not have been in the pharaonic mould, another cultural feature associated with the Nabta rulers had already set the tone for the later glories of ancient Egypt. Even at this early period, the community marked their leaders' special status in death as well as in life. Dotted around the site, archaeologists found a series of thirty mounds topped with huge stones. Their purpose is not absolutely clear, but the most likely explanation is that they marked the burials of important individuals. Already, it seems, monumental edifices were being erected for dead rulers: a tradition had begun that was to find its ultimate expression in the pyramids.

Some of the stones for these huge cairns were truly gigantic, weighing up to one-and-a-half tonnes. So, like their later counterparts at Stonehenge, they represent a huge investment of time and manpower. Even more significantly, they show that someone in the Nabta community had the authority to command and organize the necessary human resources to accomplish these feats of monumental architecture. And it was not just tombs that the Nabta people built to mark their landscape. An alignment of ten standing stones was found close to the astronomical calendar – the same combination of features that occurs at some of the major megalithic sites of northwestern Europe, such as Stonehenge and Avebury. Whether it is a cold northern climate or a hot, dry Saharan one, it seems that in situations where the environment is challenging and survival depends on critical life-and-death decisions, people respond with communal enterprise, imposing some order on their forbidding landscape through monumental feats of architecture. The resources of labour, organizational skill and physical resilience that are needed for such projects are also those that are essential for survival. In other words, two of the cornerstones of ancient Egyptian civilization – the emergence of strong leaders and the creation of huge public buildings – seem to have originated, not in the relatively easy environment of the Nile Valley, but in the challenging conditions of the dry savannah.

The sands of Nabta Playa were still to reveal one final secret. Underneath one of the large stone mounds, archaeologists were amazed to discover something altogether unexpected: not a human or animal burial, but a truly enormous sandstone boulder, carefully sculpted. Even if it dates to the latest phase of occupation, it must still pre-date the earliest known monumental sculpture from the Nile Valley by a thousand years. We cannot tell what its significance was to the people who made it, and why it should have been buried in its own 'tomb'. But the sheer effort involved in manoeuvring such a vast stone into place, shaping it to give sharp edges and smooth faces, and finally burying it under a mound of stones – this demonstrates impressive ideological motivation, social organization, and a fascination with large-scale stone-working. All three were to characterize Egyptian civilization throughout its long history.

~ · ~ · ~

*T*he discoveries at Nabta Playa have forced a major rethink of ancient Egypt's origins. The hallmarks of this great civilization seem to have begun, not among Nile Valley agriculturalists but among the cattle-herders of the dry savannahs. In this case, how is it that the uninterrupted sequence of cultural development that starts in the Badarian period seems to have begun in the Nile Valley? For was it not in towns by the banks of the river that craftsmen created the great works of art of prehistoric and dynastic Egypt? Were they not rulers from the Nile Valley that eventually became the god-like kings of the entire country? If Egyptian civilization did not spring from the floodplain, what caused this narrow ribbon of land to become the stage for such dramatic developments?

Back in the 1930s, when Winkler was first becoming interested in the Eastern Desert and its prehistoric secrets, another archaeologist working for the same patron, Sir Robert Mond, was uncovering unexpected prehistoric remains on the west bank of the Nile. The archaeologist in question was Oliver Myers, and he was excavating at the site of Armant, just south of Thebes with its impressive tombs and temples. Neither Myers nor his backer were particularly interested in finding golden treasure. Indeed, Myers clearly thought spectacular discoveries were a thing of the past: he wrote 'the cream has been skimmed off Egyptology'. To their credit, however, both men were aware of the importance of more mundane evidence for shedding light on ancient Egyptian civilization. They recognized the value of pottery, flint tools: everyday items that did not necessarily excite

14 The gold coffin of Tutankhamun. The royal regalia of crook and flail, crossed over the king's chest, hark back to the origins of ancient Egyptian civilization among semi-nomadic cattle-herders, who would have used such implements to restrain and encourage their animals.

15 A flotilla of boats, high up on the cliff face in the Wadi Barramiya. The discovery of this site was an early success of the December 2000 expedition. The inaccessibility of the petroglyphs highlights the determination and resourcefulness of the prehistoric artists.

16 Boat petroglyphs in the Wadi Barramiya. The frequent depictions of boats are perhaps the most intriguing aspect of the Eastern Desert rock art. Deciphering their meaning has shed new light on ancient Egyptian origins.

17 A flotilla of barges from the tomb of Seti I in the Valley of the Kings. Processions of boats were associated with the afterlife journey throughout the long course of ancient Eygptian civilization. The Eastern Desert rock art (such as Fig. 15) provides the earliest examples of this association.

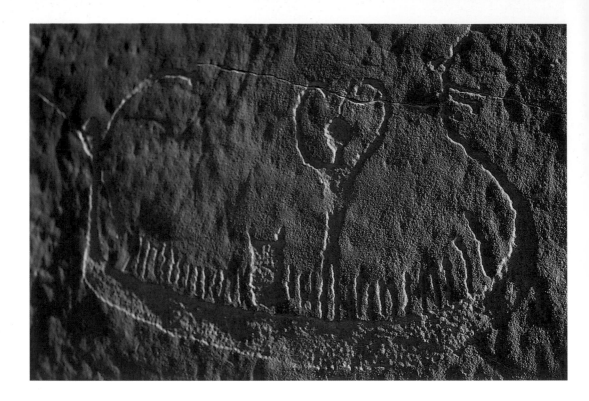

18 Petroglyph of boat and human figure in the Wadi Barramiya. Scenes like this are as powerful today as when they were first created 6,000 years ago. They give us a rare insight into the minds of Egypt's early inhabitants.

19 Boat with figures, Wadi Abu Wasil. The size and attributes of the central figures suggests that they may represent gods. If so, the idea that deities travelled by boat – which is a prominent feature of classic ancient Egyptian religion – may be of great antiquity.

20 The god Nun lifts up the boat of the rising sun – from the Papyrus of Anhai, late New Kingdom. The distinctive shape of the solar bark closely parallels boat petroglyphs in the Eastern Desert (Plate 18), suggesting that these were also transport for the gods or transfigured spirits.

21 Boat being dragged, Wadi Abu Wasil. This scene foreshadows similar ones in the Valley of the Kings, but pre-dates them by nearly three thousand years. The clues to the origins of ancient Egyptian civilization seem to lie, not in the Nile Valley, but in the inhospitable Eastern Desert.

22 The bark of the sun god dragged by attendant deities – from the tomb of Ramesses VII in the Valley of the Kings. The origins of this classic motif can now be traced back to the prehistoric period, and the rock art of the Eastern Desert.

23 Boat petroglyph, partially defaced by modern graffiti, in the Wadi Barramiya. The standing figure wearing a twin-plumed head-dress is one of the earliest depictions of a god from ancient Egypt. He points the boat towards the west, the land of the dead in ancient Egyptian religion.

24 The god Amun-Ra, on a Middle Kingdom relief in the temple of Karnak. The god is shown in typical attire, wearing the twin-plumed head-dress that identified deities in ancient Egyptian art. This convention is first attested thousands of years earlier, in the Eastern Desert rock art (Plate 23).

25 Queen Nefertari presents offerings to the goddess Isis – from the tomb of Nefertari in the Valley of the Queens. Isis wears a pair of cattle horns and carries the strangely-shaped was-sceptre which originated as a stick for use in animal husbandry. Although familiar, classic scenes of ancient Egyptian art like this one contain hidden clues about the genesis of the pharaohs.

museums and private collectors. This attention to detail was to prove a blessing to Egyptology. It was while digging in a pharaonic cemetery at Armant that Myers came across some strange-looking fragments of pottery. They were rather rough, clearly hand made, and decorated with combed and incised lines. Myers had never seen anything like them before, and thought they might be foreign. He did what any excavator would in the circumstances, and scoured the literature for parallels. He concluded that these bits of broken pots, found just beneath the surface, were connected in some way with the Sahara desert. He could not explain quite how the contacts had come about, and he did not appreciate the great antiquity of his pottery fragments; but it seemed to him that there had been a degree of interaction between desert people and valley dwellers at some stage in the past. Subsequent excavations by later generations of archaeologists would prove Myers's hunch correct. His broken pottery was prehistoric in date, and did indeed belong to the cattle-herding cultural tradition of the Western Desert. Here was proof that interaction between the savannah and the floodplain had taken place some time between 5000 and 4000 BC, when both areas played host to vibrant communities.

When later expeditions to the Western Desert found out more about its prehistoric inhabitants, some Egyptologists began to advance a radical theory: perhaps the contacts between savannah and valley people attested at Armant had, in fact, been much more common and much more widespread than this single site suggested. What if there had been increasingly frequent exchange and interaction between these two very different environments during the fifth millennium BC? Perhaps the Nile Valley had indeed proved fertile ground for the Saharan inhabitants' beliefs and practices. If cattle-herders visiting the Nile Valley on trading expeditions had also found a receptive audience for their cultural traditions, this might explain the sudden appearance at around the same time of the Badarian culture, the earliest ancestor of pharaonic civilization. Prehistoric objects from the Nile Valley decorated with scenes of savannah life seemed to add weight to the theory.

One of the most striking is a pottery object in the Royal Ontario

Museum, Toronto. Although box-like in shape, it does not look particularly like a house. It may instead represent a tent-like dwelling, the sort of temporary structure that the wandering cattle-herders of the Sahara would have carried with them as they accompanied their animals from pasture to pasture. Even more unusual than the shape of the object is its decoration. Three of the sides are incised and painted with rough sketches that bear a remarkable resemblance to the rock art of the Western Desert. They include a scene of hunting dogs, birds and a cow; and also a unique representation of two young goats suckling from their mothers. This subject-matter is unique in Predynastic art from the Nile Valley, but is closely paralleled in rock-paintings from the Uweinat region of southwestern Egypt. In general, sheep and goats figure only rarely on prehistoric Egyptian grave goods, and then most often as pot-marks (for example, on vessels from the Nagada I-period cemetery at Abadiya). By contrast, such animals are a relatively common feature in Saharan rock art. Being a unique object, the Toronto artifact is difficult to date precisely, but artistic considerations suggest the late Nagada I period, in other words around 3800 BC. The exact provenance of the object is also unknown, but it was certainly acquired in the Nile Valley. Quite how it got there remains a mystery; but the Egyptologist who has studied it believes it may have been brought to the valley by semi-nomadic pastoralists, as part of a more general population movement from the Sahara. According to this immigration theory, the gradual desiccation of the savannahs made life there increasingly difficult for herding people, and the Nile Valley increasingly attractive. When the summer rains finally became entirely unreliable, some time around 4000 BC, the cattle-herders of the Sahara left their dried-up pastures for the last time and headed for the lush grazing of the Nile Valley. They brought with them not only their cattle, but also their highly sophisticated culture – and effectively kick-started ancient Egyptian civilization.

Attractive as it may seem, there are difficulties with this theory. For a start, the Badarian culture – the remote but direct ancestor of pharaonic civilization – arose within the Nile Valley many centuries before the final desiccation of the neighbouring savannahs. So a mass immigration of Saharan cattle-herders cannot have been responsible for the earliest origins of ancient Egypt. But what if the Badarians were themselves heavily influenced by contacts with their western neighbours from the beginning? There is no denying that contacts took place; yet it would be surprising if cultural traditions were more successfully developed by people who had only just adopted them (the Badarians) than by the very people among whom these traditions originated (Saharan cattle-herders). Beliefs and practices that grew up as a response to the challenges of life in a harsh savannah environment are hardly likely to have been well suited to a very different lifestyle in the Nile Valley. Indeed, it is telling that the sort of monumental architecture seen at Nabta Playa in 4000 BC or earlier is not replicated in the Nile Valley until at least a thousand years later. Clearly, the cattle-herders of the Sahara influenced their valley-dwelling contemporaries, but by the time they moved en masse to the banks of the Nile, the development of ancient Egyptian culture in the valley was already well underway.

~·~·~

So, if the origins of ancient Egypt do not lie either in the Nile Valley or in the Western Desert, where should we look for them? To answer this question, we must first investigate the earliest Nile Valley culture in the sequence that ultimately led to pharaonic Egypt.

Until about 5000 BC, the people living by the banks of the river led a fairly sedentary existence. They relied on the abundant resources of the river itself, especially fish and shellfish. Without the need to move about in search of food, they could settle down in permanent villages. As excavated in recent times, these settlements typically comprise thick layers of occupational remains, with large quantities of pottery. All that changed dramatically at the beginning of the fifth millennium BC. A new form of subsistence appears on the scene, and with it an entirely new way of life. Archaeologists call it the Badarian culture

(Fig. 57). The first excavators to unearth evidence of the Badarians did so while digging near the small village of el-Badari, roughly half way between Cairo and Luxor. Indeed, the greatest concentration of Badarian remains have been found in the immediate vicinity, and the Badari region was probably the heartland of this particular cultural tradition. But isolated examples of Badarian pottery have also been found further afield, in southern Egypt, so the culture may have been more widespread than we tend to think. Badarian cemeteries and even a village have been excavated on the margins of the Nile floodplain, and there is no doubt that the people knew the valley and its resources well. Hippopotamus ivory was a favourite material for Badarian craftsmen. From it they fashioned beads, bracelets, spoons, even small fertility figurines. It was also a valuable material – obtaining tusks from a hippo must have been a difficult and dangerous task. So supplies of hippo ivory were no doubt carefully guarded. In one Badarian village, archaeologists found a pile of six hippo tusks in a storage pit. They must have been hidden away for future use, but something evidently happened to prevent their owner reclaiming them. The hippo itself

57 *Artifacts of the Badarian culture. In the fifth millennium BC, the Badarians were some of the first people to exploit the resources of the eastern savannah, including siltstone from the Black Mountains. They also reached the Red Sea coast and used marine shells to make jewellery.*

was an important motif in Badarian art: a rare hippo-shaped vase was found in a grave at Mostagedda, and is one of the masterpieces of pre-historic Egyptian craftsmanship. It stands at the head of a long tradition of hippo imagery in Egyptian art that lasted as long as Egyptian civilization itself.

Despite an undoubted familiarity with the Nile Valley, the Badarians were by no means restricted to this narrow strip of land. Indeed, the contents of Badarian graves display a far greater affinity with regions to the east, in other words the savannah and the Red Sea coast. Grave goods typically include a range of materials from the hills and wadis to the east of the Nile: ostrich eggs used as drinking vessels, ostrich feathers (perhaps worn in the hair for decoration), pieces of native copper and copper ore (malachite). Beads made from turquoise and steatite (soapstone) even suggest knowledge of – or at least contact with – the mountainous Sinai peninsula, to the far northeast. It is also in Badarian graves that we first encounter cosmetic palettes, the class of object that was to characterize prehistoric Egyptian culture for the next 2,000 years, right down to the formation of the state. Badarian palettes are generally rather small and simply-shaped, but some still have traces of the mineral pigments that were ground up on them, namely red ochre and green malachite, both products of the Eastern Desert. Various different hard stones were used in palette manufacture, but the favourite was siltstone from the Black Mountains of the Wadi Hammamat. The Badarian people were the first to exploit this distinctive stone, and they clearly knew where and how to obtain it. And they did not confine their visits to the Wadi Hammamat to quarrying expeditions. In 1950, a survey and excavations in the wadi by the Egyptian archaeologist Fernand Debono discovered fragments of distinctive Badarian pottery and a Badarian grave. Appropriately enough, the grave contained not one but two cosmetic palettes. Closer to the Nile Valley, near the western end of the Wadi Hammamat, Debono uncovered a prehistoric village next to the well at Laqeita (see Map 2). Numerous hearths and remains of houses contained an abundance of other cultural material: pottery, stone implements, bone objects, jewellery, small pieces of copper, even millstones. The last indicate that the inhabitants were not mere travellers, making temporary camp on their way to the siltstone quarries. Rather, they lived in the village for extended periods of time, long enough to grow cereal crops and grind them into flour. Dating of the objects showed that the village of Laqeita was first inhabited in the Badarian period. Clearly, the Badarians as a people were spread over more than just one stretch of the Nile Valley. They were also equally at home in the hills and wadis of what was then the eastern savannah. The world of the grassland was also their world, and Badarian cemeteries often include animal burials, side-by-side with human graves. As well as domesticated animals like cattle and dogs, skulls recovered from tombs include those of antelopes and jackals, very much beasts of the savannah.

From time immemorial, the Wadi Hammamat has provided the easiest, most direct route from the Nile to the Red Sea. The distance between river and coast is narrower here than at any other point in the Nile's course; and the wadi is one of the widest and most easily travelled in the whole of the Eastern Desert. So it is scarcely surprising that the Badarian people did not always stop at the Black Mountains before turning back to the valley; sometimes they continued on to the Red Sea. Jewellery made from sea shells was especially sought-after, and various species of marine mollusc are represented among Badarian grave goods: olive shells, cone shells, Nerite snails, and moon snails (genus *Natica*). The Badarians clearly maintained close contacts with the coast, and may even have settled there. For a lone grave, found already plundered in the 1920s, only 5 miles inland from the headland of Ras Samadai, contained characteristically Badarian material, including jewellery (some of it made from Red Sea shells), a bone awl, and a cosmetic palette. The palette was made of siltstone from the Black Mountains, and it still preserved traces of malachite powder. It was found together with its original grinder, a smooth quartz pebble. This grave not only demonstrates the wide geographical range of the Badarians. It also shows how easily they moved between three very different environments – river valley, savannah, and coastline – exploiting each for the resources it could offer.

The Badarians, then, were clearly a people of great dynamism. The culture they developed was the ancestor of pharaonic civilization, but it did not spring up entirely within the narrow confines of the Nile Valley. As we have seen, it drew its vitality and creativity from a range of different stimuli and environments. Rather like their cattle-herding contemporaries to the west of the Nile, the Badarians rose to the challenge of life under constantly shifting conditions. Cultural complexity was not borne of an easy agricultural lifestyle by the banks of the river, but of the fight for survival in more difficult terrain. But why did the Badarians need to leave the relative ease of the fertile Nile floodplain at all? What prompted them to travel eastwards, through wadis and hills towards the Red Sea? Like their descendants in the Nagada I period, the Badarians, too, show all the signs of a life lived on the move. Their possessions were small, light and easily portable. They showed a particular emphasis on bodily decoration: the use of palettes to grind up make-up, a fondness for hair combs and jewellery. This is a characteristic feature of semi-nomadic populations, among whom display must be expressed through the person rather than by permanent structures. The hoard of hippo tusks mentioned above also indicates a mobile lifestyle. Whoever buried the ivory clearly intended to return to the village at some future date, but needed in the meantime to leave and go elsewhere. The tusks would have been too bulky and cumbersome to carry, so they were buried with every expectation that they could be dug up again later. This is perhaps the most telling piece of evidence for the Badarians' semi-nomadic existence. It shows that they spent part of the year in villages by the banks of the Nile, returning to them on a regular basis. The other part of the year they spent elsewhere. The same story is told by the settlement remains themselves. They tend to consist of shallow layers of occupation, indicating rather brief periods of habitation interspersed by periods of abandonment. After a while, villages seem to shift their position laterally, to occupy new patches of ground. Why did the Badarians live in this way, and where did they go when they left their villages each year?

The answer to the second question is clear: the eastern savannah. The Badarians' obvious knowledge of this environment (and the Red Sea coast beyond), and the discovery of Badarian pottery and graves in the hills to the east of the Nile, leave little doubt that they spent considerable periods of time here. Why they should have done so is harder to prove, but again there is a likely explanation. As we have seen, among the animals buried in Badarian cemeteries are cattle, and there are good reasons to suppose that they were domesticated. Add that to the climatic conditions during the Badarian period – a phase of unusually high rainfall, which made the eastern savannah particularly attractive for both hunting and grazing – and it seems very likely that cattle-herding was what took the Badarians away from their Nile Valley villages on a regular basis. They combined a pastoral way of life with small-scale agriculture, whenever the opportunity arose, and a good deal of hunting. Flint arrowheads are common in the Badarian settlements that have been excavated, both Nile Valley villages and the savannah settlement at Laqeita. In other words, the pattern of life that so characterized the following Nagada I period was already established a thousand years earlier by the Badarians.

So, in the regions to the west and east of the Nile, people lived essentially the same, semi-nomadic existence from 5000 BC. But what marks out the Badarian people from their cattle-herding contemporaries in the Sahara (including the last few generations of inhabitants at Nabta Playa) is their versatility. They did not have only limited contact with the Nile Valley, like their Saharan counterparts: they actually lived in the Nile Valley for part of the year, fishing in its waters and growing crops along its banks. It was just as much a part of their domain as the eastern savannah where they hunted and herded. In other words, the Badarians bridged both worlds. As we have seen in Chapters 3 and 4, the Badarian lifestyle is very much the lifestyle of the following period as well. In its essential characteristics, the Nagada I period shows a great deal of continuity from the preceding phase. There is no sudden break, either in the way of life or in the products which have survived in the archaeological record. People still combined cattle-herding with limited agriculture, dividing their time between the valley and the savannah. The dead were accorded much the same treatment, although in the Nagada I period there is more evidence for social complexity – that is, the division of society into classes based upon political and economic power. The Badarians, too, had their leaders, as did the inhabitants of Nabta Playa; but the social divisions became rather starker in the Nagada I period, and status began to be inherited rather than acquired. Craftsmanship, already highly developed, reached new heights, probably spurred on by the patronage of wealthy rulers. Those seeds that had been planted by the Badarians were sprouting and growing fast. They would ultimately blossom spectacularly into the civilization of the pharaohs. At the heart of ancient Egypt's origins and early development lies the demanding way of life followed by the Badarians and their successors. The annual movement from Nile Valley to savannah and back again, as the people followed their all-important herds to new pastures, was a lifestyle that required adaptability, above all. It was this quality that gave the ancestors of the pharaohs a key advantage. Changes in the climate, the eventual desiccation of the savannah, a possible influx of people from the Western Desert, erratic Nile floods, growing competition for resources: none of these challenges proved insuperable because the Badarians and their descendants had developed the physical, mental and social resources to survive – to survive and to prosper.

~ · ~ · ~

To conclude our journey through space and time to the roots of ancient Egyptian civilization, let us return to the Eastern Desert rock art with which we began. We can now begin to appreciate the people who left these remarkable traces on the rocks. We understand a little more about their distinctive way of life, and the forces with which they had to contend. We can also, perhaps, sense something of the motivation behind the petroglyphs: the desire to engage with the natural and supernatural worlds in order to harness some of their power for human benefit. For, to overcome difficult and challenging conditions, divine assistance was crucial. The final wonder is not so much that the prehistoric Egyptians of 4000 BC went to such lengths to express their deepest beliefs through art, but that the symbolism they chose for this should have set the tone for the succeeding 4,000 years of ancient Egypt.

We all recognize ancient Egyptian civilization when we see it. Those distinctive hallmarks that set it apart from any other culture, ancient or modern, are instant identifiers: the plethora of gods and goddesses, many with strange animal forms; the curiously beautiful art, rich with magical and religious symbolism; a divine king presiding over everything, forming a link between gods and people. To Egyptologists working in the first half of the twentieth century this remarkable culture with its familiar strangeness seemed to have come from nowhere. It was as if the glories of ancient Egypt had suddenly been switched on like a light-bulb at the beginning of the First Dynasty; anything that came before was shrouded in primitive obscurity. This attitude partly reflected the prevailing, colonial mind-set of the time: the development of a sophisticated civilization on the 'uncivilized' continent of Africa must have been the result of conquest by a more advanced culture. It was scarcely credible – or ideologically acceptable – that the roots of ancient Egypt might lie within Egypt itself. But the uncertainty over Egyptian origins also reflected the very limited knowledge of prehistoric Egypt a hundred years ago.

It is an extraordinary fact that when Flinders Petrie, 'the father of Egyptian archaeology', first started excavating in the Nile Valley, the earliest known monuments were the great pyramids of the Fourth Dynasty. Only with the results of Petrie's pioneering excavations at Guft did material come to light that predated not only the pyramids but even the beginning of Egyptian history. Over the following two decades, Petrie and others began to reveal more and more about Egypt's remote Predynastic past; but it still seemed that there were few points of continuity with the glories of dynastic Egypt. For sure, the pottery and other objects from prehistoric graves were beautifully crafted and often finely decorated, but they still seemed a world away, both in style and quality, from the products of the pharaohs' royal workshops. How could it be that a civilization as glorious as ancient Egypt's could have had such modest beginnings? And where were the prototypes for those most distinctive of Egyptian symbols: the royal regalia, the twin plumes worn by gods, the divine boats that bore the souls of the deceased into the afterlife? None of these seemed to have any forebears in Predynastic culture. There were, of course, examples of prehistoric art – decorated pottery, a unique painted linen cloth, and a series of great, ceremonial palettes from the years immediately preceding the First Dynasty – but these showed only a restricted repertoire of symbols. Where did all the rest come from? It is little wonder that Egyptologists like Winkler felt it necessary to postulate a master race of invaders to account for the sudden appearance of classic Egyptian civilization. There were simply too many gaps in the prehistoric record to demonstrate the indigenous origins of pharaonic Egypt.

Following the upsurge of interest in Predynastic Egypt that began in the 1970s, our understanding of pharaonic origins has been transformed. There are now few people that still adhere to the 'master race' theory of old. Most Egyptologists acknowledge the significant influences that other cultures had on Egypt during its formative phases; but they recognize that, at its most fundamental, pharaonic civilization is an Egyptian, indeed an African phenomenon. And yet, there has still been a huge 'missing link' in the evolution of ancient Egypt. Scholars have had to take it on trust that some of the most characteristic elements of Egyptian art, religion and symbolism must have originated within the northeasternmost corner of Africa; but there has been no proof for this – until now. The Eastern Desert rock art described and analysed in this book represents nothing less than the discovery of that missing link. Suddenly we are faced with a dramatically different view of prehistoric Egypt. It was by no means as primitive as we thought. We can begin to glimpse its true complexity, and to chart the long course of development that ultimately led to the wonders of the pharaohs, with which we are all so familiar.

With hindsight, it was perhaps not so surprising that the missing link should have eluded us for so long. Symbols and concepts that go to the heart of a people's religion and way of life are not particularly well suited to being expressed on small, breakable objects. If we think of the western European Christian tradition (my own cultural background), the most profound and complex expressions of belief occur, not on small votive objects like candles or rosaries, but on the great canvases of religious art found in churches and cathedrals: stained glass windows and Old Master paintings of epic religious subjects. The expression of deep spiritual concerns requires special vehicles and special locations. Is it, then, so strange that the small grave goods upon which our knowledge of prehistoric Egypt has largely depended until now should not provide particularly good evidence for early Egyptian religion? What we have been missing are the prehistoric Egyptian equivalents of churches and cathedrals: the actual places where people could commune with the divine and express their most profound beliefs through the medium of art. The rock-shelters and hidden gulleys of the Eastern Desert are those very places. As we have seen, art and religion were inextricably linked in ancient Egypt. Sure enough, then, the Eastern Desert rock art also reveals the origin of many of the key elements of ancient Egyptian religious symbolism.

The afterlife journey by boat is one of the central images in the decoration of New Kingdom royal tombs in the Valley of the Kings. The transfigured spirit of the dead king is shown in the company of other souls, or alone with the gods, in a boat of special shape; the boat is dragged through the night regions of the underworld before emerging triumphant from the eastern horizon at dawn. As we have seen in Chapter 5, the association of a boat journey with the afterlife is attested archaeologically – in the form of boat burials – as early as the First Dynasty. Yet the complex symbolism showing exactly what sort of journey was envisaged seems to appear, as if from nowhere, at the beginning of the New Kingdom, some fifteen centuries later. Now, we have found its earliest expression in the rock art of the Eastern Desert. The scenes of a boat being dragged by a gang of people that occur in the Wadi Hammamat and Wadi Abu Wasil (Plate 21) precisely foreshadow the well-known New Kingdom motif (Plate 22), but at a distance of some two-and-a-half millennia. In the prehistoric examples, as in those from historic Egypt, the boat that conveys the deceased to the next world often has a large number of passengers and/or crew. Even the ruler could expect to share his craft with a crowd of other transfigured spirits. The parallels between the rock art of 4000 BC and the tomb scenes of 1500 BC are indeed striking. The discovery of the boat petroglyphs faces us with two astonishing revelations. First, the familiar ancient Egyptian concept of the afterlife originated at the very dawn of civilization in the Nile Valley, among the semi-nomadic cattle-herders whose domain encompassed both valley and savannah. Second, this concept was so powerful and so resonant that it remained unchanged throughout the succeeding thirty centuries. The longevity of Egyptian culture is as remarkable as its antiquity.

Boats were not only used to convey the dead through the next world; they were also the regular means of transport for the gods (Plate 20). Until recently, the earliest certain expression of this belief in art had been a decorated ivory comb of the First Dynasty. Now we know that the belief and its expression were far, far older. In a scene in the Wadi Barramiya, the larger-than-life cow that is being dragged along by boat almost certainly represents a deity. So, too, do the two largest figures standing in the main boat at Winkler's Site 26, in the Wadi Abu Wasil (Plate 19). These two important petroglyph sites also demonstrate the prehistoric origins of another, classic feature of ancient Egyptian civilization: the idea that deities could assume both human (anthropormorphic) and animal forms. The bizarre combination of human and animal attributes is one of the most curious, and most recognizable aspects of ancient Egyptian religion. While some deities, like the protector-goddess Hathor, were nearly always shown in animal form (in Hathor's case, as a cow), others, like the fertility and desert god Min, were most often shown as anthropomorphic. Some scholars of Egyptian religion have argued that anthropormorphic deities represent a later development; in the beginning, they suggest, gods and goddesses were generally shown in animal form. The prehistoric evidence from the Eastern Desert should be conclusive in rejecting this argument. From the very beginning, it seems, the Egyptians conceived of divinity in many different manifestations.

The two largest figures in the boat at Site 26 may also indicate a prehistoric origin for another key element of ancient Egyptian religious belief: the pairing of deities. Despite its extraordinary complexity, Egyptian religion is characterized by certain organizing principles. One of the most important is the grouping together of deities in 'families', which imposes some degree of structure on a huge and diverse pantheon. So, for example, Osiris and Isis are paired together as husband and wife; as are Amun and Mut in the New Kingdom; or Khnum and Anukis at Elephantine. Part of the underlying reasoning seems to have been that gods, particularly those imagined in human form, required consorts to fulfil their needs – which were also envisaged as human-like. It is tempting, then, to see the pairing of two superhuman, boat-borne figures as the first example of a divine couple in Egyptian religion (Plate 19). Certainly, the figures wear twin plumes in their hair, one of the classic attributes of divinity. In tombs, on temple walls, and on papyrus, the two-feathered head-dress was the mark of a god par excellence. For its origins, we now need look no further than the Eastern Desert rock art. The standing figure who points over the heads of his fellow passengers in the Wadi Barramiya is adorned with a particularly fine twin-plumed head-dress (Plate 23). So is the 'protector of cattle' depicted on the remarkable main wall at the 'jacuzzi site' in the Wadi Umm Salam. Ancient Egyptian religious iconography was not an invention of the state at the beginning of the First Dynasty. Its roots go far, far back into the prehistoric past when the Egyptians' ancestors wandered through what is now desert, stopping to record their beliefs on the rocks in sacred locations.

In the Middle and New Kingdoms the twin-plumed head-dress was associated, above all, with the god Amun, chief deity of the town of Thebes and, ultimately, of the entire Egyptian Empire (Plate 24). But in earlier periods, the twin-plumes were a marker of the god Min. Min's main cult-centre was the town of Guft, ancient Coptos, at the mouth of the Wadi Hammamat. Little surprise, then, that as well as being worshipped as a fertility god, Min should also have been regarded as patron-deity of the Eastern Desert – since expeditions into the Desert most often used Coptos as their point of departure. Most of the mining inscriptions in the Wadi Hammamat siltstone quarries refer to Min, or show him in his classic 'ithyphallic' pose: one arm upraised, holding a flail; the other grasping the root of his erect phallus. As god both of fertility and of the Eastern Desert, how appropriate it is that prayers to Min should mark the entrance to the so-called 'lovers' grotto' in the Wadi Mineh!

Besides his schoolboy appeal, Min has another claim to fame. He is the earliest individually identifiable god in ancient Egypt. Ink inscriptions of a god instantly recognizable as Min occur on Second Dynasty stone vessels. Even earlier are three colossal stone statues from the temple of Min at Coptos, discovered by Petrie during his pioneering excavations of 1894–95. Dated to the threshold of the First Dynasty, they show an unnamed ithyphallic deity who must nevertheless be the same god that is named as Min in later, historical inscriptions. These colossi push back the origins of this fascinating god to the end of pre-history. But the petroglyphs of the Eastern Desert allow us to go even further back in time. When he visited the rock-cut temple at Kanais in 1908, Arthur Weigall remarked on one of the nearby petroglyphs in particular. It shows a banana-shaped boat, of distinctive Nagada II type (one of only two certain examples from this period in the Eastern Desert rock art). The boat has three cabins. One is surmounted by some sort of awning, sheltering a human figure who may be wearing a crown. This detail is very reminiscent of one of the boats in the Painted Tomb at Nekhen, discussed in Chapter 2. The second, central cabin in the Kanais boat bears the figure of a bull, probably to be identified as a

deity or divine image in animal form. The third cabin is plain, but before it stands a figure who can be no other than the god Min. He is clearly ithyphallic with one arm in front of him and the other held aloft, brandishing a flail (Fig. 58). There can be no doubt about the god shown, and no doubt about the date of the petroglyph. Here, then, we have a recognizable and identifiable god, shown in the form he was to retain throughout the long march of Egyptian civilization, but created by an artist in the middle of the fourth millennium BC, some 500 years before the First Dynasty. However, the origins of the god Min may be even older. Close inspection of the 'protector of cattle' figure from the Wadi Umm Salam reveals that he, too, is shown in the ithyphallic pose characteristic of the fertility god (see Fig. 41). This particular example of rock art therefore holds a unique place in the story of pharaonic civilization: it is the oldest certain representation of a god from ancient Egypt.

Of course, in classic Egyptian iconography, it was not only the god Min who held a flail. The king, too, had one as part of his standard royal regalia (Fig. 59). On his golden coffin, Tutankhamun is shown with his hands crossed over his chest, holding the crook and flail (Plate 14); the

58 Boat with animals and the god Min, Kanais. This prehistoric scene from the Eastern Desert includes an early representation of the fertility god, shown in the classic form that survived throughout pharaonic times.

59 OPPOSITE The Egyptian king enthroned, holding a flail (from the macehead of King Narmer, First Dynasty). In prehistoric times, the flail was used by herders to goad and encourage their livestock. Many of the items of royal regalia carried by the pharaohs hark back to an earlier, pastoral way of life.

actual regalia that the king carried on state occasions were preserved among his burial equipment. The symbolism of the flail and crook is clear. As 'shepherd of his flock', the king needed both to encourage and to restrain his people. But why should objects associated with animal husbandry have found a central place in the paraphernalia of Egyptian kingship? Why did the sceptre carried by the gods – the so-called was-sceptre with an animal-shaped head and curious forked prongs at its base (Plate 25)– likewise begin life as something brandished by a shepherd or cow-herd? The Eastern Desert rock art reveals the answer: the origins of ancient Egyptian civilization lie among the semi-nomadic pastoralist people of the fifth and fourth millennia BC. Their lives and livelihoods depended upon their livestock. Cattle-rearing, shepherding, animal husbandry: these activities gave birth to ancient Egyptian culture, and the symbols associated with them became firmly lodged in the Egyptian consciousness. Likewise, when the king was portrayed as a wild bull, trampling his enemies underfoot, it was no mere artistic device. Rather, it expressed the awe and respect the Egyptians felt for the forces of nature, as a result of their long and intimate relationship with the natural world. When the king wore in his belt a bull's tail, he not only took on the attributes of this fierce beast. He also emphasized the central place of cattle in Egyptian culture, since time immemorial. The Narmer Palette, which stands today as an icon of early Egypt, demonstrates the predominance of cattle imagery at the dawn of Egyptian history. Not only does the king wear a bull's tail, not only is he shown in one instance as a wild bull, but the entire composition unfolds under the watchful gaze of two cattle deities. To Egyptians of 3000 BC, this symbolism must have had ancient and powerful connotations, reminding them of their own origins as a cattle-herding people.

The bull's tail suspended from the king's belt also illustrates the ancient practice of wearing animal attributes in order to take on the powers of nature. This belief goes back as far as we can trace and its earliest manifestations occur in the Eastern Desert rock art. There, the hunters don ibex horns in order to gain mastery over their quarry. Distant echoes of these prehistoric hunting expeditions in the eastern savannah are still heard 2,500 years later, when the rulers of the New Kingdom had themselves shown hunting in the very same environment. Once again, the desert hunting scenes painted in tombs, and on objects like Tutankhamun's box, can be seen as reflections of an earlier way of life: one that had imprinted itself on the Egyptian psyche.

~ · ~ · ~

*E*very state requires ideological glue to hold it together. Since time immemorial, leaders around the world have sought to unite their people by portraying those outside their society as a danger. A sense of collective identity is one of the most powerful incentives for national unity. But a sense of collective identity also requires a corresponding sense of external threat. From the very beginning of the Egyptian state – formed in about 3000 BC – the rulers of the new country were adept at this type of psychological pressure. The enemies of Egypt were presented as the enemies of creation, and it was the king's duty to crush them. Without the king as defender of order, chaos would triumph and everything would be lost. This was to prove so powerful an ideology that Egyptian kingship would survive as the sole model of government for 3,000 years – a remarkable achievement. But there was a supreme

60 *Ivory label showing the Egyptian king subjugating the desert inhabitants (reign of King Den, First Dynasty). Once Egypt had been unified into a single state, official ideology cast anyone living outside the Nile Valley as a barbarian and a threat to Egyptian culture. Ironically, this even included the pastoralists of the Red Sea hills, the very people whose distinctive lifestyle had helped to fashion pharaonic civilization.*

irony in this new, nationalistic propaganda: the outsiders vilified in official art and texts not only included the foreign peoples of Western Asia, Libya and Nubia; they also comprised the remaining pastoralist inhabitants that clung onto their ancient way of life in the hills and wadis to the east of the Nile Valley (Fig. 60). Condemned as 'barbarians' and belittled as 'sand-dwellers', these desert herdsmen were, in fact, the sole survivors of a lifestyle that had sown the seeds of ancient Egyptian civilization itself. The pharaohs' propaganda masked their own origins.

The new discoveries of rock art in the Eastern Desert have taken us on a journey of discovery, greater in its scope and more astonishing in its results than even those pioneering expeditions of Weigall and Winkler. We have dated the petroglyphs, unmasked the ancient artists, and thereby painted an unexpected picture of life in Egypt 6,000 years ago. We have also seen that the origins of pharaonic culture – its powerful art, its rich symbolism and its haunting religion – are to be found, not in a settled agricultural lifestyle by the banks of the Nile, but in the challenges of a more precarious, nomadic existence among the mountains and wadis to the east. Egypt may be the gift of the Nile; but ancient Egyptian civilization was the gift of the deserts.

POSTSCRIPT

Nearly a century has elapsed since Arthur Weigall first ventured along the Wadi Hammamat by camel, recording the petroglyphs he encountered. Yet exploration of the Eastern Desert, and its remarkable prehistoric remains, is still in its infancy. International interest in this remote and inaccessible region is growing; so is the availability of four-wheel drive vehicles in Egypt, vital for exploring the hills and wadis; but so, too, is other, more harmful activity to the east of the Nile Valley. Mining continues apace, and in increasingly remote areas. New roads are being built to provide access for miners' lorries, sections of cliff are being blasted by dynamite to reveal seams of more precious minerals; there is even talk of gold-mining being resumed at the ancient Wadi Barramiya mines. These activities are having a huge effect on the fragile desert ecosystem, and they are putting the future of the desert's prehistoric remains in great peril. Rock art sites close to major roads are particularly threatened. In the last five years alone, some of the petroglyphs along the Wadi Hammamat have disappeared due to illicit mining activity. Others in the Wadi Barramiya are being defaced by lorry drivers, who pull over for a rest on their way to and from the Red Sea. They seek out the same rock-shelters as the ancient inhabitants, but with less happy results. The need to preserve, or at the very least study, the Eastern Desert rock art is increasingly urgent. Unless action is taken very soon, many of Egypt's most remarkable treasures will be lost forever, before they have even been recorded.

Once the most endangered sites have been safeguarded for future generations, there is much more archaeological work that can and should be undertaken. So far, like the prehistoric artists, we have only scratched the surface. Where, for example, are the settlements of these ancient inhabitants? The cattle-herders left behind temporary encampments in the Nile Valley, and they must have done likewise in the eastern savannah. During my second visit to the Wadi Abu Wasil in 2000, I discovered a single fragment of red-polished pottery, typical of the Nagada I period, lying on the desert surface near Winkler's Site 26. It had almost certainly been deposited there as a result of subsequent human activity or floodwaters. And yet it hinted at the material remains of prehistoric life that must still exist in the desert, if we only knew where to look. Detailed survey work could be expected to reveal pre-historic encampments; it might also help us to understand more clearly the pattern of settlement and activity in prehistoric times. If people lived out on the savannah, they must also have died here. Strange, then, that with the exception of a few plundered Badarian graves in the Wadi Hammamat and one near the Red Sea coast, no prehistoric burials have been unearthed in the Eastern Desert. Like the camps, they may be some distance away from the major rock art sites. We need to tear our gaze away from the petroglyphs, and examine the surrounding land-scape more widely.

The origins of ancient Egypt lie in the Eastern Desert, and there is much, much more that remains to be revealed. It can only be hoped that Egyptologists will respond to the challenge, will leave behind the familiar environment of the Nile Valley, and turn their attention to the wild and forbidding regions that lie to the east. The desert still has not given up all its secrets.

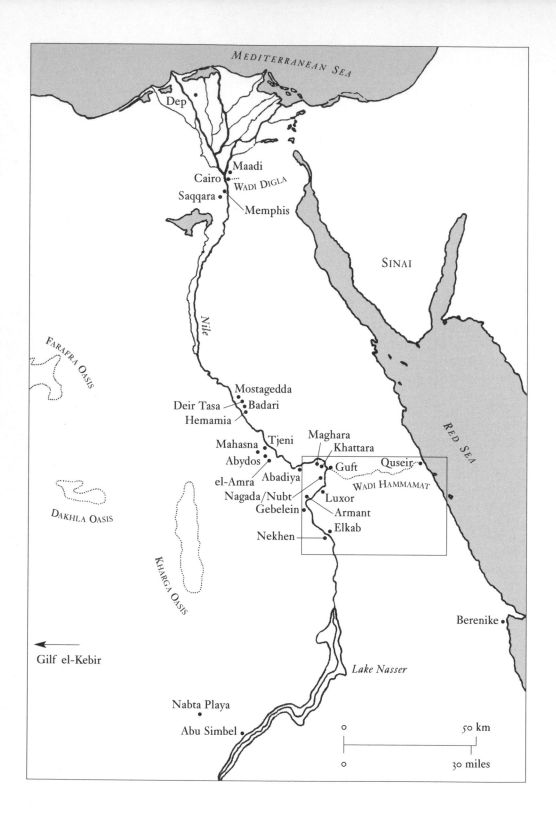

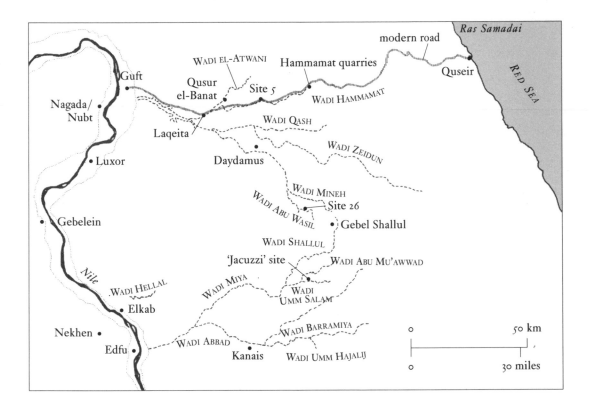

MAP 1 OPPOSITE *Egypt, showing sites referred to in the text.*

MAP 2 *The Eastern Desert showing sites referred to in the text. The modern tourist city of Luxor is shown for reference.*

The Nile Valley and the Deserts in Prehistory

Approximate Date BC	Archaeological Period	Main Developments		
		Western Savannah	Nile Valley	Eastern Savannah
5000	Badarian	Major period of settlement at Nabta Playa already well underway	First farmers grow seasonal crops	Exploitation of silstone quarries in the Black Mountains begins
4500			Beginnings of social complexity, leading to hereditary chiefs by Nagada I	Frequent contacts between the Nile valley and the Red Sea via the Wadi Hammamat
4000	Nagada I	Contacts between savannah and valley communities at Armant		Settlement at the well of Laqeita
			Major period of hunting, herding and rock art by semi-nomadic communities	
3500	Nagada II		Consolidation of territories around Tjeni, Nubt and Nekhen	
	Nagada III	Gradual drying out: savannah becomes desert	Political unification of Egypt	Gradual drying out: savannah becomes desert
3000				

BIBLIOGRAPHY AND GUIDE TO FURTHER READING

CHAPTER 1

Weigall's expeditions

Weigall, A. E. P. (1909) *Travels in the Upper Egyptian Deserts*. Edinburgh and London: William Blackwood and Sons.

Winkler's expeditions

Winkler, H. A. (1937) *Völker und Völkerbewegungen im vorgeschichtlichen Oberägypten im Lichte neuer Felsbilder*. Stuttgart: W. Kohlhammer Verlag.

—— (1938) *Rock-drawings of Southern Upper Egypt*, Vol. 1. London: Egypt Exploration Society.

Červíček, P. (1986) *Rock Pictures of Upper Egypt and Nubia*. Rome: Herder. Istituto Universitario Orientale, Napoli. Supplemento 46 agli annali.

Other expeditions (in chronological order)

Golenischeff, W. (1890) 'Une excursion à Bérénice', *Recueil de Travaux relatifs à la Philologie et à l'Archéologie Égyptiennes et Assyriennes* 13.

Frobenius, L. (1927) 'Die Forschungen in die nubische Wüste', *Mitteilungen des Forschungsinstitut für Kulturmorphologie* 2.

Dunbar, J. H. (1941) *The Rock-pictures of Lower Nubia*. Cairo: Government Press.

Resch, W. F. E. (1963) 'Neue Felsbilderfunde in der ägyptische Ostwüste', *Zeitschrift für Ethnologie* 88: 86–97.

—— (1967) *Die Felsbilder Nubiens*. Graz: Akademische Druck und Verlagsanstalt.

Váhala, F. and P. Červíček (1999) *Katalog der Felsbilder aus der tschechoslowakischen Konzession in Nubien*. Prague: Karls-Universität Prag, Verlag Karolinum.

Redford, S. and D. Redford (1989) 'Graffiti and petroglyphs old and new from the Eastern Desert', *Journal of the American Research Center in Egypt* 26: 3–49.

Herbert, S. and H. Wright (1988/89) 'Report on the 1987 University of Michigan/University of Assiut expedition to Coptos and the Eastern Desert', *Newsletter of the American Research Center in Egypt* 143/144: 1–4.

Fuchs, G. (1989) 'Rock engravings in the Wadi el-Barramiya, Eastern Desert of Egypt', *The African Archaeological Review* 7: 127–54.

—— (1991) 'Petroglyphs in the Eastern Desert of Egypt: new finds in the Wadi el-Barramiya', *Sahara* 4: 59–70.

Rohl, D. (ed.) (2000) *The Followers of Horus. Eastern Desert Survey Report*, Vol. 1. Basingstoke: ISIS.

CHAPTER 2

Methods of dating rock art

Bednarik, R. G. (2001) 'Breakthrough in dating Australian Ice Age rock art', *Minerva* 2001: 2–3.

Berger, M. A. (1992) 'Predynastic animal-headed boats from Hierakonpolis and southern Egypt' in R. Friedman and B. Adams (eds) *The*

Followers of Horus. Studies Dedicated to Michael Allen Hoffman, 107–20. Oxford: Oxbow Monograph 20. Egyptian Studies Association Publication No. 2.

Červíček, P. (1974) Felsbilder des Nord-Etbai, Oberägyptens und Unternubiens. Wiesbaden: Franz Steiner Verlag.

Chippindale, C. and P. S. C. Taçon (eds) (1998) The Archaeology of Rock-art. Cambridge: Cambridge University Press.

Davis, W. (1978a) 'Dating prehistoric rock drawings in Upper Egypt and Nubia', Current Anthropology 19: 216–17.

—— (1978b) 'Towards a dating of prehistoric rock-drawings in Upper Egypt and Nubia', Journal of the Society for the Study of Egyptian Antiquities 8: 25–34 and 84–5.

—— (1984) 'The earliest art in the Nile valley', in L. Krzyzaniak and M. Kobusiewicz (eds) Origin and Early Development of Food-producing Cultures in North-eastern Africa, 81–94. Poznan: Polish Academy of Sciences and Poznan Archaeological Museum.

Huyge, D. (1984) 'Rock drawings at the mouth of Wadi Hellal, Elkab (Upper Egypt)', in L. Krzyzaniak and M. Kobusiewicz (eds) Origin and Early Development of Food-producing Cultures in North-eastern Africa, 231–4. Poznan: Polish Academy of Sciences and Poznan Archaeological Museum.

—— (2002) 'Dating the El-Hosh rock art', Egyptian Archaeology 20: 34–5.

Muzzolini, A. (1992) 'Dating the earliest central Saharan rock art: archaeological and linguistic data', in R. Friedman and B. Adams (eds) The Followers of Horus. Studies Dedicated to Michael Allen Hoffman, 147–54. Oxford: Oxbow Monograph 20. Egyptian Studies Association Publication No. 2.

Also Redford and Redford (1989); Resch (1967); and Winkler (1937).

Climatic conditions in prehistory

Butzer, K. W. (2001) 'Desert environments', in D. B. Redford (ed.) The Oxford Encyclopedia of Ancient Egypt, 385–9. New York: Oxford University Press.

Comparative archaeological material

Ayrton, E. R. and W. L. S. Loat (1911) Pre-dynastic Cemetery at El Mahasna. London: Egypt Exploration Fund. Memoir 31.

Brunton, G. (1937) Mostagedda and the Tasian Culture. London: Quaritch. British Museum Expedition to Middle Egypt, first and second years 1928, 1929.

Brunton, G. and G. Caton-Thompson (1928) The Badarian Civilisation and Predynastic Remains Near Badari. London: British School of Archaeology in Egypt/Quaritch.

Garstang, J. (1902) Mahâsna and Bêt Khallâf. London: British School of Archaeology in Egypt.

Myers, O. H. (1933) 'Two prehistoric objects', Journal of Egyptian Archaeology 19: 55.

Petrie, W. M. F. (1901) Diospolis Parva. The Cemeteries of Abadiyeh and Hu 1898–9. London: Egypt Exploration Fund.

—— (1920) Prehistoric Egypt. London: British School of Archaeology in Egypt/Quaritch.

Petrie, W. M. F. and J. E. Quibell (1896) Naqada and Ballas. London: Quaritch.

Randall-MacIver, D. and A. C. Mace (1902) El Amrah and Abydos 1899–1901. London: Quaritch.

Tutundžić S. P. (2000) 'Predynastic potmarks in the shape of boats', *Discussions in Egyptology* 48: 95–113.

CHAPTER 3

Andrews, C. (1994) *Amulets of Ancient Egypt*. London: British Museum Press; Austin: University of Texas Press.

Close, A. E. (1990) 'Living on the edge: Neolithic herders in the Eastern Sahara', *Antiquity* 64: 79–96.

Hoffman, M. A. (1984) *Egypt Before the Pharaohs. The Prehistoric Foundations of Egyptian Civilization*. London: Ark Paperbacks.

Wendorf, F., A. E. Close and R. Schild (1989) 'Early domestic cattle and scientific methodology', in L. Krzyzaniak and M. Kobusiewicz (eds) *Late Prehistory of the Nile Basin and the Sahara*, 61–7. Poznan: Poznan Archaeological Museum.

Wengrow, D. (2001) 'Rethinking 'cattle cults' in early Egypt: towards a prehistoric perspective on the Narmer Palette', *Cambridge Archaeological Journal* 11: 91–104.

Also Resch (1967) and Winkler (1937).

CHAPTER 4

Midant-Reynes, B. (translated by I. Shaw) (2000) *The Prehistory of Egypt. From the First Egyptians to the First Pharaohs*. Oxford: Blackwell.

CHAPTER 5

Interpretations of Egyptian rock art

Hassan, F. (1992) 'Primeval goddess to divine king. The mythogenesis of power in the early Egyptian state', in R. Friedman and B. Adams (eds) *The Followers of Horus. Studies Dedicated to Michael Allen Hoffman*, 307–21. Oxford: Oxbow Monograph 20. Egyptian

Studies Association Publication No. 2.

Wilkinson, T. (2000) 'Rock drawings of the Eastern Desert', in D. Rohl (ed.) *The Followers of Horus. Eastern Desert Survey Report*, Vol. 1, 158–65. Basingstoke: ISIS.

Williams, B. (1988) *Decorated Pottery and the Art of Naqada III. A Documentary Essay*. Munich: Deutscher Kunstverlag. Münchner Ägyptologische Studien 45.

Also Červíček (1974) and Wengrow (2001).

Parallels from other rock art traditions

Francfort, H.-P. (1998) 'Central Asian petroglyphs: between Indo-Iranian and shamanistic interpretations', in C. Chippindale and P. S. C. Taçon (eds) *The Archaeology of Rock-art*, 302–18. Cambridge: Cambridge University Press.

Klassen, M. A. (1998) 'Icon and narrative in transition: contact-period rock-art at Writing-On-Stone, southern Alberta, Canada', in C. Chippindale and P. S. C. Taçon (eds) *The Archaeology of Rock-art*, 42–72. Cambridge: Cambridge University Press.

Ouzman, S. (1998) 'Towards a mindscape of landscape: rock-art as expression of world-understanding', in C. Chippindale and P. S. C. Taçon (eds) *The Archaeology of Rock-art*, 30–41. Cambridge: Cambridge University Press.

Whitley, D. S. (1998) 'Finding rain in the desert: landscape, gender and far western North American rock-art', in C. Chippindale and P. S. C. Taçon (eds) *The Archaeology of Rock-art*, 11–29. Cambridge: Cambridge University Press.

CHAPTER 6

Davies, V. and R. Friedman (1998) *Egypt*. London: British Museum Press.

Debono, F. (1951) 'Expedition archéologique royale au desert oriental (Keft–Kosseir): rapport préliminaire sue la campagne 1949', *Annales du Services des Antiquités de l'Egypte* 51: 59–110.

Majer, J. (1992) 'The Eastern Desert and Egyptian prehistory', in R. Friedman and B. Adams (eds) *The Followers of Horus. Studies Dedicated to Michael Allen Hoffman*, 227–34. Oxford: Oxbow Monograph 20. Egyptian Studies Association Publication No. 2.

Malville, J. McK., F. Wendorf, A. A. Mazar and R. Schild (1998), 'Megaliths and Neolithic astronomy in southern Egypt', *Nature* 392: 488–91.

McHugh, W. (1990) 'Implications of a decorated Predynastic terracotta model for Saharan Neolithic influence in the Nile valley', *Journal of Near Eastern Studies* 49: 265–80.

Murray, G. W. and D. E. Derry (1923) 'A Predynastic burial on the Red Sea coast of Egypt', *Man* 23: 129–31.

Resch, W. F. E. (1964) 'Eine vorgeschichtliche Grabstätte auf dem Ras Samadai', *Mitteilungen der Anthropologischen Gesellschaft in Wien* 93/94: 119–21.

Wendorf, F. and A. E. Close (1992) 'Early Neolithic food-economies in the eastern Sahara', in R. Friedman and B. Adams (eds) *The Followers of Horus. Studies Dedicated to Michael Allen Hoffman*, 155–62. Oxford: Oxbow Monograph 20. Egyptian Studies Association Publication No. 2.

Also Hoffman (1984) and Midant-Reynes (2000).

SOURCES OF ILLUSTRATIONS

The line drawings of rock art have, in all cases, been taken from photographs and not collated from the original petroglyphs. Rather than being precise scale drawings, the illustrations are intended to present the reader with clear images of some of the most important art from the Eastern Desert.

TEXT FIGURES
Unless otherwise indicated, the figures are by Kate Spence.

1, 3 From A. E. P. Weigall (1909) *Travels in the Upper Egyptian Deserts*. Edinburgh and London: William Blackwood and Sons.

5 From W. M. F. Petrie (1920) *Prehistoric Egypt*. London: British School of Archaeology in Egypt/Quaritch.

6 BELOW Kate Spence (after E. R. Ayrton and W. L. S. Loat (1911) *Pre-dynastic Cemetery at El Mahasna*, plate XXVII.13. London: Egypt Exploration Fund).

7 From C. Aldred (1965) *Egypt to the End of the Old Kingdom*, fig. 27. London: Thames & Hudson Ltd.

8, 9 From W. M. F. Petrie and J. E. Quibell (1896) *Naqada and Ballas*, plate XXIX. London: Quaritch.

10, 11 From Petrie, op. cit.

12 From J. E. Quibell and F. W. Green (1902) *Hierakonpolis*, II, plate LXXIX. London: Quaritch.

13 From Petrie, op. cit.

14 Kate Spence (after G. Brunton (1937) *Mostagedda and the Tasian Culture*, pl. XXXVIII. London: Quaritch).

15 From Petrie and Quibell, op. cit., plate LI.

16 From D. Randall MacIver and A. C. Mace (1902) *El-Amrah and Abydos 1899–1901*, plate XII. London: Quaritch.

18, 19 From Petrie, op. cit.

20 BELOW Kate Spence (after G. Dreyer (1998), in *Mitteilungen des Deutschen Archäologischen Instituts, Abteilung Kairo* 54: 113).

21 Kate Spence (after Dreyer, op. cit., 114).

23, 24 Kate Spence (after H. A. Winkler (1938) *Rock-drawings of Southern Upper Egypt*, I. London: Egypt Exploration Society).

26 From Petrie and Quibell, op. cit., plate LI.

27 From W. M. F. Petrie (1901) *Diospolis Parva. The Cemeteries of Abadiyeh and Hu 1898–9*, plate V. London: Egypt Exploration Society.

28 Ashmolean Museum, Oxford.

30 Kate Spence (after Rohl (ed.) (2000) *The Followers of Horus. Eastern Desert Survey Report*, Vol. I, 163. Basingstoke: ISIS).

31 From Petrie and Quibell, op. cit., plate XXIX.

35 From Randall MacIver and Mace, op. cit., plate IX.

36 From W. M. F. Petrie (1920) *Prehistoric Egypt*. London: British School of Archaeology in Egypt/Quaritch.

46 Kate Spence (after K. M. Cialowicz, in R. Friedman and B. Adams (eds) (1992) *The Followers of Horus. Studies Dedicated to Michael Allen Hoffman*, fig. 6. Oxford: Oxbow).

50 Araldo de Luca/Archivio White Star.

54 From Weigall, op. cit.

55 Kate Spence (after Rohl (ed.), op. cit., 147).

56 Kate Spence (after D. Wengrow (2001), in *Cambridge Archaeological Journal* 11: fig. 3).

57 British Museum, London.

58 From Weigall, op. cit.

60 British Museum, London.

PLATES

Unless otherwise indicated, the plates are the author's own photographs, taken in the field.

12 Egyptian Museum Turin.

14, 17 Araldo de Luca/Archivio White Star.

19 Kate Spence.

20 British Museum, London.

21 Kate Spence.

22 Aidan Dodson.

25 Araldo de Luca/Archivio White Star.

INDEX

Numerals in *italics* refer
to text illustration
numbers; numerals in
bold refer to plate
numbers.

Abadiya 89–91, 93, 95, 101,
    124, 178
Abu Kua 20
Abu Rawash 156
Abydos 13–14, 76–8;
    pilgrimage to 148
agriculture 115–16, 163,
    184–5
amulets 100, *34*
Amun 191, **24**
Arab conquest 59, 61
Armant 94, 168, 177
Australian rock art 55–6,
    62, 137, 158

Badari 101, 180
Badarian culture 62, 84,
    92, 97, 164, 168, 177,
    178–85, 197, *57*
Bedouin 24, 44, 45, 61–2, **2**
Berenike 26
Beni Hasan 31
Bir Shallul 43, 44
Bir Umm Fawakhir 123
Black Mountains 13, 15,
    17, 20, 29, 91–2, 120, 181
boats: as transport for
    afterlife journey 148–50,
    152–4, 156–8, *53, 54, 55,*
    23; as transport for gods
    150–2, *51, 52,* **19, 20**; being
    dragged 151, 188–9, *52, 21,*
    22; flotillas of 49, 68,
    86, 158, *11, 12, 15, 17*

'Canyon of the Boats' *see*
    Wadi Umm Salam
carnelian 90, 125
cattle 102, *35, 36,* **7**; burials
    101, 166, 184; -herding
    104–12, 165–6, 177–9,
    184–5, *37, 38, 39, 40, 41,*
    symbolism 99–101, 103,
    138–9, 140, 155, 193–4, *31,*
    32, 33, 34, 52, 56, **25**
Červíček, Pavel 28, 30
child burials 77, 107, 121
climate, ancient 44, 46,
    52, 59–61, 67, 104–5, 113,
    162, 184
combs 88, 89, 112, 143, 150,
    27, 46
copper 126, 181
Coptos *see* Guft
crocodile 67, 73, 87, 88,
    114, *16*

Davis, Whitney 58
Daydamus Roman fort 46
Debono, Fernand 181–2
Deir Tasa 94
Delta 115, 119, 125–7, 163
Den, King *60*
Dep 127
diet 116–17, 129, 135
dogs, hunting- 65–6, 87,
    95, 140, *7, 8, 9,* **6**
'Dirwa-people' 76, 83, 85
Djet, King 48
Dunbar, J. H. 27, 56, 57
'dynastic race' 30, 68 (*see*
    also 'Eastern Invaders')

Eastern Desert landscape
    12, **1**

'Eastern Invaders' 25, 30,
    68, 71, 84–5, 147–8
Egypt Exploration Fund
    (*later* Egypt
    Exploration Society) 8,
    14, 24
el-Amra 72–3, 101, 102
elephant 59, 63, 87, 92, 113,
    125, *3, 26*
elevation as an indicator
    of date 58
Elkab 17, 160
Emery, Bryan 147

'feather-diadem people'
    (Federschmuck-Leute)
    83–5
Frobenius, Leo 26
Fuchs, Gerard 28–9, 48

galena 91–2
gazelle 44, 59, 87, 88, 113,
    116, *28*
Gebelein 101, 124 (*see also*
    linen)
Gebel el-Arak knife-
    handle 71–2
Gebel Shallul 43–4
giraffe 52, 59, 66, 67, 73,
    87, 113, 132, 146, *10, 16,* **4**
gold mines, Eastern
    Desert 43, 123, 196
Golenischeff 13
Guft 20, 21, 160, 186, 191

Hatshepsut, King 31–2,
    151
head-dress, twin-plumed
    52, 139, 141–3, 190, *41, 53,*
    19, 23, 24, 25

Hemamia 93
Herbert, Sharon 29
Herodotus 162
hippopotamus 72, 86, 87, 88, 91, 92, 114, 132, 180–1, *5, 16*; hunting 50, 64–5, 81, 95, 136, 139, *6*
hunting rituals 95–6, 159, *30, 44*

ibex 45, 57, 59, 66, 87, 88, 92, 132, 141, 143–4, *47*, **8**
irrigation 115
Isis 190, **25**
ivory 120, 180

Kanais 18, 41–2, 191; rock art 67, 69, 105, 153, 155, 158, *3, 54, 58*
Khasekhemwy, King 149, 156
Khattara 93
Khufu, King 149, 156

Laqeita 182, 184
linen, painted 63, 65, 74, 158, **12**
location as an indicator of date 57

Maadi 126
mace 79, 107, *21, 22, 60*
Maghara 94
Mahasna 64–5, 70, 76, 101
malachite 92, 125, 181, 182
map, ancient 50–1, *2*
'master race' 25, 30, 147 (*see also* 'dynastic race', Eastern Invaders)
Memphis 101, 163
Mersa Alam 29, 42
Mesopotamia 25, 71–2, 84, 94, 147–8
microerosion analysis 56
Min 190, 191–2, *41, 58*
Mond, Sir Robert 18, 168

Mostagedda 65, 71
Myers, Oliver 168, 177

Nabta Playa 164–8, 184–5
Nagada 62, 66, 71, 81–2, 88, 90 (*see also* Nubt); period 62–3
Narmer, King 79, 99–100, 193, *33, 59*
Nazi ideology 19–20, 21, 84
Nekhen 69, 97, 101, 118, 119, 124–5, 128 (*see also* Painted Tomb)
Nubt 123–5 (*see also* Nagada)

Osiris 148–9, 190
ostrich 48, 95, 113, 132, 142–3, 145, 151, *29, 45, 49, 50, 51*; eggs 90, 124, 125, 181, *27, 28*

Painted Tomb 63, 69, 79, 143, 158, 191, *12*
Palestinians 126–7
palette, cosmetic 91–2, 94–5, 112, 119–20, 181–3, *27, 29*
patination 56–7
'penis-sheath people' (Penistaschen -Leute) 83–5
Petrie, Flinders 13, 30, 54, 63, 72, 186–7, 191
pot-marks 71, 88, 178, *15, 26*
pottery: C-ware 63, 70–1, 74, 75, 76, 78, 87, *5, 6, 7, 8, 9, 10, 13, 14, 18, 19, 31, 32, 36*; D-ware 68, *11*; manufacture 97–99, 117–18
Predynastic period 63
Pyramid Texts 148–9, 156

Quseir 20
Qusur el-Banat 17, 21, 29

Ra 149–50
radiocarbon dating 55
Ras Samadai 182
red crown 22, 80–2, *23, 24, 25*
Redford, Donald & Susan 29, 58–9
Red Sea 87, 181–3
regalia, royal 139, 192–3, *59*, **14**, **25** (*see also* red crown)
Resch, Walther 26, 84–5
rock paintings 23, 178
Rohl, David 30, 68, 69, 71, 148; desert expeditions *7, 31*

Saqqara 101, 156
settlements 93–4, 121, 122–3, 179, 182
shamans 121–2, 128, 131, 137–8, *43*
Speos Artemidos 31
'standard people' (Standarten-Leute) 83–4
stars, symbolism of 47, 157–8, **9**
stone-working 118–19, 168

Thutmose III, King 100
Tjeni 123
tomb decoration 103, 135–7
Tutankhamun, King 9, 18, 26; objects from the tomb of 140, 192–3, *50*, **14**

UNESCO missions in Nubia 26, 27, 58

Váhala, František 27–8
Valley of the Kings 9, 10, 18, 26, 149, 154, 188, **17**, **22**
Verner, Miroslav 27

Wadi Abbad 124, 129
Wadi Abu Mu'awwad
108–9, 1; rock art 108,
157–8, *39*
Wadi Abu Wasil 22, 60;
rock art 65, 67, 71, 75, 79,
106–7, 108, 144, 150–1,
160, 189, *22, 37, 38, 43, 44,
48, 51,* **8**; Site 26 45, 105,
137, 197, **11, 19, 21**
Wadi Barramiya 17, 26,
28–9, 42, 124, 196; rock
art 64, 65, 73, 105, 142,
151, 152–3, 155, 158, 160,
190, *6, 45, 52, 53, 5,* **6, 15,
16, 18, 23**
Wadi Digla 126
Wadi el-Atwani 21, 86;
rock art 67, 78, 154, 161,
20, 55, **10**

Wadi Hammamat 13, 15,
20, 21, 29, 123, 182, 196
(*see also* Black
Mountains, Laqeita);
mining inscriptions 58,
191; rock art 69–70, 155,
157, 160, 189, **9**
Wadi Hellal 26
Wadi Mineh 22, 44–5, 86,
191, 3; rock art 139, 145,
4, 42, 49, **4**
Wadi Miya 26, 29, 49
Wadi Qash 22; Site 18 22,
46, 81–2, *23, 24*
Wadi Shallul 43
Wadi Umm Salam 47,
50–3, 60; 'jacuzzi' site
53, 67, 74, 110–11, 139,
146, 190; rock art 57, 58,
73, 75, 105, 108, 142, 144,

160, 192, *2, 17, 40, 41, 47,*
7, 13
Wadi Zeidun 22, 44, 60
'wedge-shaped people'
(Keilstil-Leute) 76,
83–5, *19*
Weigall, Arthur 13–14,
147, 191, *1*, desert
expeditions 14–18, 195,
196
Western Desert 23,
177–9
Winkler, Hans 13, 18–20,
25–6, 28, 57–8, 61, 68, 71,
76, 83, 147, 168, 187;
desert expeditions 21–4,
45, 195; notebooks 8, 24
Wright, Henry 29

Žába, Zbyněk 27–8